Legends
of
Our Time

Legends of Our Time

by Elie Wiesel

Schocken Books · New York

First published by Schocken Books 1982

10 9 8 7 6 5 4   87 88

Published by agreement with Elirion Associates

Portions of this book have appeared in *Commentary,*
Hadassah Magazine, and *Jewish Heritage*

Library of Congress Cataloging in Publication Data
Wiesel, Elie, 1928–
  Legends of our time.
  Translation of: Le chant des morts.
  Reprint. Originally published: 1st ed. New
York: Holt, Rinehart and Winston, 1968.
  I. Title.
[PQ2683.I32C513 1982]   843'.914   82–3225   AACR2

Designer: Robert Sugar

Manufactured in the United States of America
ISBN 0–8052–0714–7

CONTENTS

Introduction

The old white-bearded Rebbe looked at me disapprovingly. "So, it's you," he sighed, "you are Dodye Feig's grandson." He had recognized me at once, which both pleased and embarrassed me. I have not been so identified since my childhood; since the war.

Twenty years have elapsed since he last saw me. We were still in Hungary. My mother brought me to him to obtain his blessing. Now we were alone in the room, in a suburb near Tel Aviv. And for some reason I felt more uncomfortable than then.

He sat in his armchair and studied me. He had not changed much. His face remained friendly and pained. His smile contained all the wisdom in the world.

"Hmmm, Dodye Feig's grandson," the Rebbe repeated as if to himself. His eyes were resting upon me and I wondered whom he saw. And why he turned sad all of a sudden. Then I realized that unlike him I have changed in more than one way; I was no longer his disciple.

"Rebbe," I said, "I have been working hard to acquire a name for myself. Yet, to you I am still attached to my grandfather's." It was a poor attempt to break the tension; it failed. Now he seemed somewhat angry: "So, that's what you have been doing all these years," he remarked. He nodded his head and added: "What a pity."

My mother's father was among his favorite followers. Dodye Feig was more famous as a Hasid than his grandson shall ever be as a writer. Was that the reason for the Rebbe's anger? I dared not ask him. I became again in his presence the child I once was who would only listen.

"Tell me what you are doing," the Rebbe said in a soft voice. I told him I was writing. "Is that all?" he asked in disbelief. I said, yes, that's all. His expression was so re-

proachful that I had to elaborate and explain that some writings could sometimes, in moments of grace, attain the quality of deeds. He did not seem to understand.

I was afraid of that. If I had waited so many years before I came to see him—although I knew where he could be found—it was because I did not want to acknowledge the distance between us. I was afraid both of its existence and its absence. All the words that for twenty years I have been trying to put together, were they mine or his? I did not have the answer but, somehow, I was afraid that he did.

"What are you writing?" the Rebbe asked. "Stories," I said. He wanted to know what kind of stories: true stories. "About people you knew?" Yes, about people I might have known. "About things that happened?" Yes, about things that happened or could have happened. "But they did not?" No, not all of them did. In fact, some were invented from almost the beginning to almost the end. The Rebbe leaned forward as if to measure me up and said with more sorrow than anger: "That means you are writing lies!" I did not answer immediately. The scolded child within me had nothing to say in his defense. Yet, I had to justify myself: "Things are not that simple, Rebbe. Some events do take place but are not true; others are—although they never occurred."

That was all I could say. Was it enough? I did not know. The Rebbe let it stand. He stared at me for a long moment until his face lit up again. He asked me to come closer; I obeyed. "Come," he said, "Dodye Feig's grandson should not go away empty-handed. Come and I shall give you my blessing."

And I did not dare remind him that for so many years I have tried so hard to acquire for myself a name which needed to be blessed, too. Only after I had left him did I realize that perhaps the time has come for Dodye Feig's grandson to take my place at the typewriter.

Legends
of
Our Time

1.

The Death
of My Father

The anniversary of the death of a certain Shlomo ben Nissel falls on the eighteenth day of the month of *Shvat*. He was my father, the day is tomorrow; and this year, as every year since the event, I do not know how to link myself to it.

Yet, in the *Shulchan Aruch*, the great book of precepts by Rabbi Joseph Karo, the astonishing visionary-lawmaker of the sixteenth century, precise, rigorous rules on the subject do exist. I could and should simply conform to them. Obey tradition. Follow in the footsteps. Do what everyone does on such a day: go to the synagogue

three times, officiate at the service, study a chapter of
Mishna, say the orphan's *Kaddish* and, in the presence of
the living community of Israel, proclaim the holiness of
God as well as his greatness. For his ways are tortuous
but just, his grace heavy to bear but indispensable, here
on earth and beyond, today and forever. May his will be
done. Amen.

This is undoubtedly what I would do had my father
died of old age, of sickness, or even of despair. But such is
not the case. His death did not even belong to him. I do
not know to what cause to attribute it, in what book to
inscribe it. No link between it and the life he had led. His
death, lost among all the rest, had nothing to do with
the person he had been. It could just as easily have
brushed him in passing and spared him. It took him
inadvertently, absent-mindedly. By mistake. Without
knowing that it was he; he was robbed of his death.

Stretched out on a plank of wood amid a multitude of
blood-covered corpses, fear frozen in his eyes, a mask of
suffering on the bearded, stricken mask that was his face,
my father gave back his soul at Buchenwald. A soul useless in that place, and one he seemed to want to give
back. But, he gave it up, not to the God of his fathers, but
rather to the impostor, cruel and insatiable, to the enemy
God. They had killed his God, they had exchanged him
for another. How, then, could I enter the sanctuary of the
synagogue tomorrow and lose myself in the sacred repetition of the ritual without lying to myself, without lying to
him? How could I act or think like everyone else, pretend
that the death of my father holds a meaning calling for
grief or indignation?

Perhaps, after all, I should go to the synagogue to
praise the God of dead children, if only to provoke him
by my own submission.

Tomorrow is the anniversary of the death of my father
and I am seeking a new law that prescribes for me what
vows to make and no longer to make, what words to say
and no longer to say.

In truth, I would know what to do had my father, while alive, been deeply pious, possessed by fervor or anguish of a religious nature. I then would say: it is my duty to commemorate this date according to Jewish law and custom, for such was his wish.

But, though he observed tradition, my father was in no way fanatic. On the contrary, he preached an open spirit toward the world. He was a man of his time. He refused to sacrifice the present to an unforeseeable future, whatever it might be. He enjoyed simple everyday pleasures and did not consider his body an enemy. He rarely came home in the evening without bringing us special fruits and candies. Curious and tolerant, he frequented Hasidic circles because he admired their songs and stories, but refused to cloister his mind, as they did, within any given system.

My mother seemed more devout than he. It was she who brought me to *heder* to make me a good Jew, loving only the wisdom and truth to be drawn from the Torah. And it was she who sent me as often as possible to the Rebbe of Wizsnitz to ask his blessing or simply to expose me to his radiance.

My father's ambition was to make a man of me rather than a saint. "Your duty is to fight solitude, not to cultivate or glorify it," he used to tell me. And he would add: "God, perhaps, has need of saints; as for men, they can do without them."

He could be found more often in government offices than in the synagogue—and, sometimes, in periods of danger, even more often than at home. Every misfortune that befell our community involved him directly. There was always an impoverished, sick man who had to be sent in an emergency to a clinic in Kolozsvar or Budapest; an unfortunate shopkeeper who had to be bailed out of prison; a desperate refugee who had to be saved. Many survivors of the Polish ghettos owed their lives to him. Furnished with money and forged papers, thanks to him and his friends, they were able to flee the country for

Rumania and from there to the United States or Palestine. His activities cost him three months in a Hungarian prison cell. Once released, he did not utter a word of the tortures he had undergone. On the very day of his release, he took up where he had left off.

My mother taught me love of God. As for my father, he scarcely spoke to me about the laws governing the relations between man and his creator. In our conversations, the *Kaddish* was never mentioned. Not even in camp. Especially not in camp.

So I do not know what he would have hoped to see me do tomorrow, the anniversary of his death. If only, in his lifetime, he had been a man intoxicated with eternity and redemption.

But that is not the problem. Even if Shlomo ben Nissel had been a faithful servant of the fierce God of Abraham, a just man, of demanding and immaculate soul, immune against weakness and doubt, even then I would not know how to interpret his death.

For I am ignorant of the essentials: what he felt, what he believed, in that final moment of his hopeless struggle, when his very being was already fading, already withdrawing toward that place where the dead are no longer tormented, where they are permitted at last to rest in peace, or in nothingness—what difference does it make?

His face swollen, frightful, bloodless, he agonized in silence. His cracked lips moved imperceptibly. I caught the sounds, but not the words of his incoherent memory. No doubt, he was carrying out his duty as father by transmitting his last wishes to me, perhaps he was also entrusting me with his final views on history, knowledge, the world's misery, his life, mine. I shall never know. I shall never know if he had the name of the Eternal on his lips to praise him—in spite of everything—or, on the contrary, because of everything, to free himself from him.

Through puffy, half-closed eyelids, he looked at me and, at times, I thought with pity. He was leaving and it pained him to leave me behind, alone, helpless, in a world he had hoped would be different for me, for himself, for all men like him and me.

At other times, my memory rejects this image and goes its own way. I think I recognize the shadow of a smile on his lips: the restrained joy of a father who is leaving with the hope that his son, at least, will remain alive one more minute, one more day, one more week, that perhaps his son will see the liberating angel, the messenger of peace. The certitude of a father that his son will survive him.

In reality, however, I do not hesitate to believe that the truth could be entirely different. In dying, my father looked at me, and in his eyes where night was gathering, there was nothing but animal terror, the demented terror of one who, because he wished to understand too much, no longer understands anything. His gaze fixed on me, empty of meaning. I do not even know if he saw me, if it was me he saw. Perhaps he mistook me for someone else, perhaps even for the exterminating angel. I know nothing about it because it is impossible to grasp what the eyes of the dying see or do not see, to interpret the death rattle of their last breath.

I know only that that day the orphan I became did not respect tradition: I did not say *Kaddish*. First, because no one there would have heard and responded "Amen." Also because I did not yet know that beautiful and solemn prayer. And because I felt empty, barren: a useless object, a thing without imagination. Besides there was nothing more to say, nothing more to hope for. To say *Kaddish* in that stifling barracks, in the very heart of the kingdom of death, would have been the worst of blasphemies. And I lacked even the strength to blaspheme.

Will I find the strength tomorrow? Whatever the answer, it will be wrong, at best incomplete. Nothing to do with the death of my father.

The impact of the holocaust on believers as well as unbelievers, on Jews as well as Christians, has not yet been evaluated. Not deeply, not enough. That is no surprise. Those who lived through it lack objectivity: they will always take the side of man confronted with the Absolute. As for the scholars and philosophers of every genre who have had the opportunity to observe the tragedy, they will—if they are capable of sincerity and humility—withdraw without daring to enter into the heart of the matter; and if they are not, well, who cares about their grandiloquent conclusions? Auschwitz, by definition, is beyond their vocabulary.

The survivors, more realistic if not more honest, are aware of the fact that God's presence at Treblinka or Maidanek—or, for that matter, his absence—poses a problem which will remain forever insoluble.

I once knew a deeply religious man who, on the Day of Atonement, in despair, took heaven to task, crying out like a wounded beast, "What do you want from me, God? What have I done to you? I want to serve you and crown you ruler of the universe, but you prevent me. I want to sing of your mercy, and you ridicule me. I want to place my faith in you, dedicate my thought to you, and you do not let me. Why? Why?"

I also knew a free-thinker, who, one evening, after a selection, suddenly began to pray, sobbing like a whipped child. He beat his breast, became a martyr. He had need of support, and, even more, of certitude: if he suffered, it was because he had sinned; if he endured torment, it was because he had deserved it.

Loss of faith for some equaled discovery of God for others. Both answered to the same need to take a stand, the same impulse to rebel. In both cases, it was an accusation. Perhaps some day someone will explain how, on the level of man, Auschwitz was possible; but on the level of God, it will forever remain the most disturbing of mysteries.

Many years have passed since I saw my father die. I have grown up and the candles I light several times a year in memory of departed members of my family have become more and more numerous. I should have acquired the habit, but I cannot. And each time the eighteenth day of the month of *Shvat* approaches, I am overcome by desolation and futility: I still do not know how to commemorate the death of my father, Shlomo ben Nissel, a death which took him as if by mistake.

Yes, a voice tells me that in reality it should suffice, as in previous years, to follow the trodden path: to study a chapter of *Mishna* and to say *Kaddish* once again, that beautiful and moving prayer dedicated to the departed, yet in which death itself figures not at all. Why not yield? It would be in keeping with the custom of countless generations of sages and orphans. By studying the sacred texts, we offer the dead continuity if not peace. It was thus that my father commemorated the death of his father.

But that would be too easy. The holocaust defies reference, analogy. Between the death of my father and that of his, no comparison is possible. It would be inadequate, indeed unjust, to imitate my father. I should have to invent other prayers, other acts. And I am afraid of not being capable or worthy.

All things considered, I think that tomorrow I shall go to the synagogue after all. I will light the candles, I will say *Kaddish,* and it will be for me a further proof of my impotence.

2.
My Teachers

For some, literature is a bridge linking childhood to death. While the one gives rise to anguish, the other invites nostalgia. The deeper the nostalgia and the more complete the fear, the purer, the richer the word and the secret.

But for me writing is a *matzeva*, an invisible tombstone, erected to the memory of the dead unburied. Each word corresponds to a face, a prayer, the one needing the other so as not to sink into oblivion.

This is because the Angel of Death too early crossed my childhood, marking it with his seal. Sometimes I think I see him, his look victorious, not at the end of the journey but at its starting point. He fuses into the very beginning, the first élan, rather than into the abyss which cradles the future.

Thus, I evoke the solitary victor with nostalgia, almost without fear. Perhaps this is because I belong to an uprooted generation, deprived of cemeteries to visit the day after the New Year, when, according to custom, we fall across the graves and commune with our dead. My generation has been robbed of everything, even of our cemeteries.

I left my native town in the spring of 1944. It was a beautiful day. The surrounding mountains, in their verdure, seemed taller than usual. Our neighbors were out strolling in their shirt-sleeves. Some turned their heads away, others sneered.

After the war I had several opportunities to return. Temptation was not lacking, each reasonable: to see which friends had survived, to dig up the belongings and valuable objects we had hidden the night before our departure, to take possession once again, even fleetingly, of our property, of our past.

I did not return. I began to wander across the world, knowing all the while that to run away was useless: all roads lead home. It remains the only fixed point in this seething world. At times I tell myself that I have never really left the place where I was born, where I learned to walk and to love: the whole universe is but an extension of that little town, somewhere in Transylvania, called Màrmarosszighet.

Later, as student or journalist, I was to encounter in the course of my wanderings strange and sometimes inspiring men who were playing their parts or creating them: writers, thinkers, poets, troubadours of the apocalypse. Each gave me something for my journey: a phrase, a wink, an enigma. And I was able to continue.

But at the moment of *Heshbon-Hanefesh,* of making an

accounting, I recognize that my real teachers are waiting, to guide and urge me forward, not in awesome, distant places, but in the tiny classrooms filled with shadows and with song, where a boy I used to resemble still studies the first page of the first tractate of the Talmud, certain of finding there answers to all questions. Better: all answers *and* all questions.

Thus, the act of writing is for me often nothing more than the secret or conscious desire to carve words on a tombstone: to the memory of a town forever vanished, to the memory of a childhood in exile, to the memory of all those I loved and who, before I could tell them I loved them, went away.

My teachers were among them.

The first was an old man, heavy-set, with a white beard, a roguish eye and anemic lips. His name escapes me. In fact, I never knew it. In town, people referred to him as "the teacher from Betize," doubtless because he came from the village of that name. He was the first to speak to me lovingly about language. He put his heart and soul into each syllable, each punctuation mark. The Hebrew alphabet made up the frame and content of his life, contained his joys and disappointments, his ambitions and memories. Outside the twenty-two letters of the sacred tongue, nothing existed for him. He would say to us with tenderness: "The Torah, my children, what is it? A treasure chest filled with gold and precious stones. To open it you need a key. I will give it to you, make good use of it. The key, my children, what is it? The alphabet. So repeat after me, with me, aloud, louder: *Aleph, bet, gimmel!* Once more, and again, my children, repeat with force, with pride: *Aleph, bet, gimmel.* In that way the key will forever be part of your memory, of your future: *Aleph, bet, gimmel.*"

It was "Zeide the Melamed" who later taught me Bible and, the following year, Rashi's commentaries. Eternally in mourning, this taciturn teacher, with his bushy black beard, filled us with uneasiness mixed with fear. We thought him severe if not cruel. He never hesitated to rap the knuckles of anyone who came late or distorted the meaning of a sentence. "It's for your own good," he used to explain. He was quick to fly into a rage and whenever he did we lowered our heads and, trembling, waiting for the lull. But he was, in truth, a tormented and sentimental man. While punishing a recalcitrant pupil he suffered; he did not allow it to show because he did not want us to think him weak. He revealed himself only to God. Why was so much slander spread about him? Why was he credited with a meanness he did not have? Perhaps because he was hunchbacked, because he lowered his eyes when he spoke. The children, who unwittingly frightened him, liked to believe that ugliness is the ally of meanness if not its expression.

His school was in a ramshackle house, at the end of the court, and consisted of only two rooms. He held forth in the first. In the other, his assistant, a young scholar named Itzhak, opened for us the heavy doors of the Oral Tradition. We began with the tractate of *Baba-Metzia:* it dealt with a dispute between two persons who found a garment, to whom did it belong? Itzhak read a passage and we repeated it in the customary *niggun.* By the end of the semester we were able to absorb an entire page a week. Next year came the study of the *Tossafot,* which comment on the commentaries. And our brains, slowly sharpening, pierced the meaning of each word, released the illumination it has contained for as long as the world has been world. Who came closest to that light: the school of Shammai, the intransigent? or that of Hillel, his interlocutor and rival? Both. All trees are nourished by the same sap. Yet I felt closer to the House of Hillel; it strove to make life more tolerable, the quest more worthwhile.

At the age of ten I left Itzhak and became a student of the "Selishter Rebbe," a morose character with wild eyes, a raucous, brutal voice. In his presence no one dared open his mouth or fall into daydream. He terrorized us. Whenever he distributed slaps—which happened often, and often for no reason—he did so with all his strength; and he had strength to spare. That was his method of enforcing discipline and preparing us for the Jewish condition.

At twilight, between *Minhah* and *Maariv* prayers, he used to force us to listen as he read a chapter from the literature of *Mussar*. As he described the tortures suffered by the sinner in his grave, even before appearing before the heavenly tribunal, sobs would shake his entire body. He would stop and bury his head in his hands. It was as if he experienced the pangs of the last judgment in advance. I shall never forget his detailed descriptions of hell which, in his naïveté, he situated in a precise spot, in the heavens.

On the Sabbath he became a different person, almost unrecognizable. He made his appearance at the synagogue opposite the Little Market. Standing next to the stove to the right of the entrance, looking hunted, he lost himself in prayer, seeing no one. I would greet him but he did not respond. He would not hear me. It was as if he no longer knew who I was, or that I was there at all. The seventh day of the week he consecrated to the creator and he saw nothing of what surrounded him, not even himself. He prayed in silence, apart; he did not follow the cantor, his lips scarcely moved. A distant sadness hovered over his distracted gaze. Weekdays, I was less afraid of him.

I had decided to change schools and I became the student of three successive teachers; they too were natives of nearby villages.

Their attitude was more humane. We already considered ourselves "grownups" who could take on a *sugya,* even a difficult passage, without assistance. Every now and then, when at an impasse, we would ask them to show us how to continue; the moment the problems posed in the commentaries of the *Marsha* or the *Maharam* were unraveled, their swift clarity dazzled us. To emerge suddenly from the entanglement of a Talmudic thought always brought me intense joy; each time I would find myself on the threshold of a luminous, indestructible universe, and I used to think that over and beyond the centuries and the funeral-pyres, there is always a bridge that leads somewhere.

Then the Germans invaded our little town and the nostalgic singing of the pupils and their teachers was interrupted. To hear it once more, I would give all I possess, all that has been promised me.

From time to time I sit down again with a tractate of the Talmud. And a paralyzing fear comes over me: it is not that I have forgotten the words, I would still know how to translate them, even to comment on them. But to speak them does not suffice: they must be sung and I no longer know how. Suddenly my body stiffens, my glance falters, I am afraid to turn around: behind me my masters are gathered, their breath burning, they are waiting, as they did long ago at examination time, for me to read aloud and demonstrate to the past generations that their song never dies. My masters are waiting and I am ashamed to make them wait. I am ashamed, for they have not forgotten the song. In them the song has remained alive, more powerful than the forces that annihilated them, more obstinate than the wind that scattered their ashes. I want to plead with them to return to their graves, no longer to interfere with the living. But they have nowhere to go; heaven and earth have rejected them. And so, not to humiliate them, I force myself to read a first sentence, then I reread it in order to open it, close it again, before joining it to the next. My voice does not rise above a murmur. I have betrayed them: I no longer know how to sing.

With but a single exception, all my masters perished in the death factories invented and perfected for the glory of the national German genius.

I saw them, unshaved, emaciated, bent; I saw them make their way, one sunny Sunday, toward the railroad station, destination unknown. I saw "Zeide the Melamed," his too-heavy bundle bruising his shoulders. I was astonished: to think that this poor wanderer had once terrorized us. And the "Selishter Rebbe," I saw him too in the middle of the herd, absorbed in his own private world as if in a hurry to arrive more quickly. I thought: his face has taken on the expression of Shabbat, and yet it is Sunday. He was not weeping, his eyes no longer shot forth fire; perhaps at last he was going to discover the truth— yes, hell does exist, just as this fire exists in the night.

And so for the tenth time I read the same passage in the same book, and my masters, by their silence, indicate their disapproval: I have lost the key they entrusted me.

Today other books hold me in their grip and I try to learn from other storytellers how to pierce the meaning of an experience and transform it into legend. But most of them talk too much. Their song is lost in words, like rivers in the sand.

It was the "Selishter Rebbe" who told me one day: "Be careful with words, they're dangerous. Be wary of them. They beget either demons or angels. It's up to you to give life to one or the other. Be careful, I tell you, nothing is as dangerous as giving free rein to words."

At times I feel him standing behind me, rigid and severe. He reads over my shoulder what I am trying to say; he looks and judges whether his disciple enriches man's world or impoverishes it, whether he calls forth angels, or on the contrary kneels before demons of innumerable names.

Were the "Selishter Rebbe" with his wild eyes not standing behind me, I should perhaps have written these lines differently; it is also possible that I have written nothing.

Perhaps I, his disciple, am nothing more than his tombstone.

3.

The Orphan

My first friend was an orphan. That is about all I remember about him. I have forgotten his name, how he looked, what he was like. The color of his eyes, the rhythm of his walk: these too, forgotten. Did he like to sing, to laugh, to play in the sun, to roll in the snow? I cannot remember and, sometimes, I feel a vague remorse, as if it were a rejection.

I sometimes search my memory hoping to find him again, to save him, or, at least, to restore to him a face, a past: I emerge empty-handed. While I have no difficulty seeing myself as a child again, he, the orphan, remains unreachable: an echo without voice, a shadow without reflection. Of our friendship, all that has been preserved is the sadness his presence inspired in me. Even now, discovering the orphan in each human being is enough to reopen an old wound, never fully healed.

I must have been five, maybe a little older. I had scarcely begun to go to primary school, to *heder*. Among the children whom I did not know and did not want to know, I felt myself to be, like each of them, no doubt, the victim of my parents' injustice. I made up countless illnesses so that I could stay home with my mother for just one more day, to hear her say she still loved me, that she was not going to turn me over to strangers.

Obstinate, I resisted the efforts of my old white-bearded schoolmaster, who gently persisted in wanting to teach me the Hebrew alphabet. I think it was because, like all children, I preferred remaining a child. I dreaded the universe of rigid laws which I sensed were inside those black letters whose mysterious power seizes hold of the imagination like a defenseless prey. Whoever says *a* will say *b* and before one notices it, one is already caught up in the machinery: one begins to find words satisfying, one makes gods of them. I had an obscure premonition that, once this threshold were crossed, it would be the letters of the alphabet that would, in the end, undo my innocence, impose itself between my desires and their realization.

The other pupils, as recalcitrant as I, showed the same distrust. Only the orphan was of a different breed. He never acted spoiled; he never tried the patience and kindness of our teacher. First to arrive, he was always the last to leave. He was not rowdy, he did not have tantrums. Diligent, obedient, in contrast to us, he did not feel uprooted in the narrow room with its damp walls, that room where we spent endless hours around a rectangular table, worn down by three generations of unhappy schoolboys.

His exemplary behavior could only annoy us: why did

he insist on being different? After a while, I understood:
he *was* different. His mother had died giving birth to
him.

I did not know then what it meant to die. In fact, to be
an orphan had, in my eyes, a kind of distinction, an honor
that did not fall to everyone. Secretly, I began to envy
him. Yet my attitude toward him changed. To win his
trust, I shared my possessions with him, my little snacks,
my presents. At home no one understood: all of a sudden
I, who refused to eat at every meal, began carrying off
double portions.

My mother was alive and that seemed to me unjust.
When I was with the orphan, I felt at fault: I possessed
a wealth denied to him. And neither one of us had anything to do with it. I would have given everything to
restore the balance. To redeem myself, I was ready to
become not only his debtor but his admirer as well, his
benefactor. For his part, he accepted my sacrifices, and I
no longer remember if he thanked me for them, if he
really needed them. I do not know why, but I thought he
was poor. Or rather—yes, I do know why: spoiled child
that I was, I saw every orphan as a *poor* orphan. I could
not conceive of misfortune except in its totality: whoever
lost one portion of affection, one possibility of love, lost
everything.

His birthday coinciding with the anniversary of his
mother's death, I heard him saying *Kaddish* in the synagogue. I had to restrain myself with all my might to keep
from tearing myself away from my father and rushing
over to my friend to embrace him, weeping, and repeat
with him word by word the prayer which gives praise to
God, who must know what he is doing when he takes
away the joy of little children.

Over the years our paths separated. The orphan went
his own way. I made new friends, and today I have
other reasons for assuming my share of guilt, but at the
root of this feeling it is always him I find.

Still, I know very well that my first friend long ago ceased to be a unique case: we all belong to a generation of orphans, and the *Kaddish* has become our daily prayer. But each time death takes someone away from me, it is him, my forgotten friend, I mourn. Sometimes I wonder if he did not have my face, my fate perhaps, and if he was not already what I was about to become. Then I tell myself that I should set myself to learning the alphabet, diligently, if only to resemble him the more.

My memory proves more faithful to the other friends who followed the orphan: Haimi Kahan, Itzu Yunger, Yerachmiel Mermelstein, Itzu Goldblat. Yerachmiel disappeared in the war; Itzu Yunger survived him only to die a few years later in New York. From Paris I had written him of my intention to visit him; too late. I had mailed my letter to a dead friend.

Haimi Kahan now lives in Brooklyn. Itzu Goldblat has gone to live in Israel. We see each other rarely. We hardly write one another, except for banalities, the usual good wishes for the New Year. At times, I meet one or the other, and then the present vanishes: *do you remember?* Yes, I remember. A short, embarrassed silence and that is all. Actually, that is enough. Childhood, after all, is only a source which acquires depth with the years; the further away one is from it, the more one benefits from its purity if not its freshness. How can one remain forever thirsty? There is no answer anymore: that, too, has drowned in the source.

During our rare meetings, Haimi Kahan and I like to recall an adventure into which we once threw ourselves with all the ardor of our thirteen years. We had decided to found our own synagogue, our own school, where young people could pray and study among themselves. At six o'clock every morning, Haimi's father—Nochem Hersh, the Chief Rabbi's secretary and tutor—gave us instruction in the Talmud, revealing to us its rigor and dazzling beauty. For us, the written law and the Oral

Tradition represented the only possible safeguard. As long as we were engaged in the deep study of the tractates of *Baba-Kama* (the First Door) or *Baba-Batra* (the Last Door), as long as we earnestly read a few chapters of Psalms before and after the morning prayer, nothing bad could happen to us.

Events took it upon themselves to demonstrate the opposite. The Germans occupied the town and we had to close down our meeting room. Nochem Hersh left us for the ghetto. But his melodious voice still vibrates in my own every time I open the Talmud and submit to its laws, breathe within its closed system and steep myself in its splendor. Today, I would be inclined to admit that Nochem Hersh was right, but not entirely: the Torah contains the reflection of truth if not its flame; but it does not constitute a safeguard, especially not in terms of humanity. Today I believe I have proof that the Torah itself has become an orphan.

With Itzu Goldblat, a goldsmith and the son of a goldsmith, I shared an ambition as naïve as it was boundless: to hasten the coming of the Messiah. We were obsessed by it. Caught up in the Kabbala and its practices, we used our free time to mortify our bodies by fasting and our thoughts by silence. Determined to obtain in dream the "Gilui Eliyahu," a meeting with the prophet Elijah, the herald of deliverance, we came to forget the reality of a world at war. Only internal fulfillment concerned us. Our incantations went on for hours. In the street they took us for sleepwalkers. Before every service, we made our way to the *mikvah*, to the ritual baths, to purify ourselves, otherwise our pleas would never reach their destination. Sometimes, seized with mad exaltation we thought we could almost hear the footsteps of the Messiah: soon the goal would be reached, the sound of the *shofar*, the prophet's own trumpet, would shock the very heart of history and the blood of victims would no longer flow; soon our enemies, struck with humility and repentance, would realize that they would never succeed in annihilating the people of the covenant by slaughtering its children. Soon, but when? We were burning with impatience, time pressed, we had to hurry. Once again the German occupation put an end to our dream and—who knows?—perhaps to our work as well. The executioner arrived before the Messiah and somewhere, under the peaceful skies of Silesia, the eternal people with all that it embodied was consumed in flames, day and night, especially night, for nothing.

Of all my friends, Yerachmiel, was the one who refused to live on illusions. He fastened on to concrete things, tangible, realizable. He had discovered political Zionism and from then on he could not hold himself back. Without neglecting his Talmudic studies, he found the time to collect money for the Jewish National Fund, and never missed an opportunity to propagate his ideas among the young. A talented agitator, he appeared wherever he could find an audience. He got excited when he spoke, but in his speeches he appealed to reason rather than to that sense of nostalgia which every Jew must feel for Zion.

On Saturday afternoons, for the third traditional meal of Shabbat, he came to our small synagogue and spoke to us not about the Bible or the weekly *Sedra*, but about the situation in Palestine. That is how I learned that the Holy Land was under British mandate and that an underground Jewish movement had taken up arms to win independence.

Although I remained closed to the political aspects of his talks, I was won over by his enthusiasm. Every time he mentioned the name of Jerusalem, of Safed, of Mount Carmel, the blood rushed to my head: was it really possible, then, to reconstruct the Temple and the kingdom of David other than through penitence and tears? And God, what was his place in all this? Yerachmiel had an answer for everything. At his instigation, I began to learn modern

Hebrew. He had managed to dig up, I have no idea where, a grammar book and he was never without it. He lent it to me for a week and I had to swear to him that I would watch over it as though it were the apple of my eye. Before returning this precious work to him, I had learned it all by heart and still today I can remember whole pages.

But Yerachmiel's path led him far from Jerusalem the majestic, far from romantic Galilee. He left in the first transport. I followed him as far as the gates of the ghetto. Lost in the crowd, he did not notice me. He was dreaming. Of what? Of the Jewish national renaissance? Of the Hebrew resistance at the time of the Roman occupation? Like everyone else, he was carrying a bundle over his shoulder. I think I know what was in it. Besides food and clothing, an irreplaceable little Hebrew grammar.

Later on, among the post-war ruins, in France, in Israel, and in other places, I became friendly with this or that person long enough to walk a few steps on the road together. But the adventures which marked the beginning of my life—never again would I know their intensity, their burning.

I have grown older and today I know the value of words, of waiting. All roads lead to man; and he continues to wander from one desert to another. And the source, a mirage at dusk, moves further and further into the distance. Whoever claims to hear the footsteps and the heartbeat of the Messiah hears only the footsteps and stifled outcries of my friends, who left the country of my childhood, where the insatiable beast who devours our dead right down to the soul crouched in wait for them.

No use retracing my footsteps, looking for a trace of the orphan all the way back to the house of my first teacher. I already know the alphabet.

4.

An Evening Guest

Like all the persecuted Jewish children, I passionately loved the prophet Elijah, the only saint who went up to heaven alive, in a chariot of fire, to go on through the centuries as the herald of deliverance.

For no apparent reason, I pictured him as a Yemenite Jew: tall, somber, unfathomable. A prince ageless, rootless, fierce, turning up wherever he is awaited. Forever on the move, defying space and nature's laws. It is the end which attracts him in all things, for he alone comprehends its mystery. In the course of his fleeting visits, he consoles the old, the orphan, the abandoned widow. He moves across the world, drawing it in his wake. In his eyes he holds a promise he would like to set free, but he has neither the right nor the power to do so. Not yet.

In my fantasy I endowed him with the majestic beauty of Saul and the strength of Samson. Let him lift his arm, and our enemies would fling themselves to the ground. Let him shout an order, and the universe would tremble: time would run faster so that we might arrive more quickly at the celestial palace where, since the first day of creation, and, according to certain mystics, long before that, the Messiah has awaited us.

A Yemenite Jew, I no longer know why. Perhaps because I had never seen one. For the child I then was, Yemen was not to be found on any map but somewhere else, in the kingdom of dreams where all sad children, from every city and every century, join hands to defy coercion, the passing years, death.

Later on, I saw the prophet and had to admit my error. He was a Jew, to be sure, but he came from no farther away than Poland. Moreover, he had nothing about him of the giant, the legendary hero. Pitiful, stoop-shouldered, he tightened his lips when he looked at you. His movements betrayed his weariness, but his eyes were aflame. One sensed that, for him, the past was his only haven.

It was the first night of Passover. Our household, brightly lit, was preparing to celebrate the festival of freedom. My mother and my two older sisters were bustling about the kitchen, the youngest was setting the table. Father had not yet returned from synagogue.

I was upset: we were going to partake of the ritual meal with only just the family, and I would have preferred having a guest as in preceding years. I recovered my good mood when the door opened and father appeared, accompanied by a poorly dressed, shivering, timid stranger. Father had approached him in the street with the customary phrase: *Kol dichfin yetei veyochal* (Let him who is hungry come eat with us).

"I'm not hungry," the stranger had answered.

"That makes no difference; come along anyway. No one should remain outside on a holiday evening."

Happy, my little sister set another place. I poured the wine.

"May we begin?" my father asked.

"Everything is ready," my mother answered.

Father blessed the wine, washed his hands, and prepared to tell us, according to custom, of the exploits of our ancestors, their flight from Egypt, their confrontation with God and their destiny.

"I'm not hungry," our guest said suddenly. "But I've something to say to you."

"Later," my father answered, a bit surprised.

"I haven't time. It's already too late."

I did not know that this was to be the last *Seder*, the last Passover meal we would celebrate in my father's house.

It was 1944. The German army had just occupied the region. In Budapest the Fascists had seized power. The Eastern front was at Körösmezö, barely thirty kilometers from our home. We could hear the cannon fire and, at night, the sky on the other side of the mountains turned red. We thought that the war was coming to an end, that liberation was near, that, like our ancestors, we were living our last hours in bondage.

Jews were being abused in the streets; they were being humiliated, covered with insults. One rabbi was compelled to sweep the sidewalk. Our dear Hungarian neighbors were shouting: "Death to the Jews!" But our optimism remained unshakable. It was simply a question of holding out for a few days, a few weeks. Then the front would shift and once again the God of Abraham would save his people, as always, at the last moment, when all seems lost.

The *Haggadah*, with its story of the Exodus, confirmed

our hope. Is it not written that each Jew must regard
himself, everywhere and at all times, as having himself
come out of Egypt? And that, for each generation, the
miracle will be renewed?

But our guest did not see things that way. Disturbed,
his forehead wrinkled, he troubled us. Moody and irritated, he seemed intent upon irritating us as well.

"Close your books!" he shouted. "All that is ancient
history. Listen to me instead."

We politely concealed our impatience. In a trembling
voice, he began to describe the sufferings of Israel in the
hour of punishment: the massacre of the Jewish community of Kolomai, then that of Kamenetz-Podolsk. Father
let him speak, then resumed the ancient tale as though
nothing had happened. My little sister asked the traditional four questions which would allow my father, in his
answers, to explain the meaning and import of the holiday. "Why and in what way is this night different from all
other nights?" "Because we were slaves under Pharaoh,
but on this night God made us free men." Discontent with
both the question and the answer, our guest repeated
them in his own way: "Why is this night not different
from other nights? Why this continuity of suffering? And
why us, always us? And God, why doesn't he intervene?
Where is the miracle? What is he waiting for? When is he
going to put himself between us and the executioners?"

His unexpected interruptions created a feeling of uneasiness around the table. As soon as one of us opened his
mouth, our guest would cut us short:

"You concern yourselves with a past that's three thousand years old and you turn away from the present:
Pharaoh is not dead, open your eyes and see, he is de-
stroying our people. Moses is dead, yes, Moses is dead, but
not Pharaoh: he is alive, he's on his way, soon he'll be at
the gates of this city, at the doors of this house: are you
sure you'll be spared?"

Then, shrugging his shoulders, he read a few passages

from the *Haggadah:* in his mouth, the words of praise became blasphemies.

Father tried to quiet him, to reassure him: "You're downhearted, my friend, but you must not be. Tonight we begin our holiday with rejoicing and gratitude."

The guest shot him a burning glance and said: "Gratitude, did you say? For what? Have you seen children butchered before their mother's eyes? I have, I've seen them."

"Later," said my father. "You'll tell us all about that later."

I listened to the guest and kept wondering: who is he? what does he want? I thought him sick and unhappy, perhaps mad. It was not until later that I understood: he was the prophet Elijah. And if he bore little resemblance to the Elijah of the Bible or to the prophet of my dreams, it is because each generation begets a prophet in its own image. In days of old, at the time of the kings, he revealed himself as a wrathful preacher setting mountains and hearts on fire. Then, repentant, he took to begging in the narrow streets of besieged Jerusalem, to emerge, later as student in Babylonia, messenger in Rome, beadle in Mayence, Toledo, or Kiev. Today, he had the appearance and fate of a poor Jewish refugee from Poland who had seen, too close and too many times, the triumph of death over man and his prayer.

I am still convinced that it was he who was our visitor. Quite often, of course, I find it hard to believe. Few and far between are those who have succeeded in seeing him. The road that leads to him is dark and dangerous, and the slightest misstep might bring about the loss of one's soul. My Rebbe would cheerfully have given his life to catch one glimpse of him, if only for the span of a lightning flash, a single heartbeat. How then had I deserved what is refused so many others? I do not know. But I maintain that the guest was Elijah. Moreover, I had proof of this soon afterward.

Tradition requires that after the meal, before prayers are resumed, a goblet of wine be offered the prophet Elijah, who, that evening, visits all Jewish homes, at the same moment, as though to emphasize the indestructibility of their ties with God. Accordingly, Father took the beautiful silver chalice no one ever used and filled it to the brim. Then he signaled my little sister to go to the door and ask the illustrious visitor to come taste our wine. And we wanted to tell him: you see, we trust you; in spite of our enemies, in spite of the blood that has been shed, joy is not deserting us, we offer you this because we believe in your promise.

In silence, aware of the importance of the moment, we rose to our feet to pay solemn tribute to the prophet, with all the honor and respect due him. My little sister left the table and started toward the door when our guest suddenly cried out:

"No! Little girl, come back! I'll open the door myself!"

Something in his voice made us shudder. We watched him plunge toward the door and open it with a crash.

"Look," he cried out, "there's no one there! No one! Do you hear me?"

Whereupon he leaped out and left the door wide open.

Standing, our glasses in our hands, we waited, petrified, for him to come back. My little sister, on the brink of tears, covered her mouth with both hands. Father was the first to get hold of himself. In a gentle voice he called out after our guest: "Where are you, friend? Come back!"

Silence.

Father repeated his call in a more urgent tone. No reply. My cheeks on fire, I ran outside, sure I would find him on the porch: he was not there. I flew down the steps: he could not be far. But the only footsteps that resounded in the courtyard were my own. The garden? There were many shadows under the trees, but not his.

Father, Mother, my sisters, and even our old servant,

not knowing what to think, came out to join me. Father said: "I don't understand."

Mother murmured: "Where can he be hiding? Why?"

My sisters and I went out into the street as far as the corner: no one. I started shouting: "H-e-e-y, friend, where are you?" Several windows opened: "What's going on?"

"Has anyone seen a foreign Jew with a stooped back?"

"No."

Out of breath, we all came together again in the court-yard. Mother murmured: "You'd think the earth swallowed him up."

And Father repeated: "I don't understand."

It was then that a sudden thought flashed through my mind and became certainty: Mother is mistaken, it is the sky and not the earth that has split open in order to take him in. Useless to chase after him, he is not here any-more. In his fiery chariot he has gone back to his dwelling-place, up above, to inform God what his blessed people are going to live through in the days to come.

"Friend, come back," my father shouted one last time. "Come back, we'll listen to you."

"He can't hear you anymore," I said. "He's a long way off by now."

Our hearts heavy, we returned to the table and raised our glasses one more time. We recited the customary blessings, the Psalms, and, to finish, we sang *Chad Gadya*, that terrifying song in which, in the name of justice, evil catches evil, death calls death, until the Angel of De-struction, in his turn, has his throat cut by the Eternal himself, blessed-be-he. I always loved this naïve song in which everything seemed so simple, so primitive: the cat and the dog, the water and the fire, first executioners then victims, all undergoing the same punishment within the same scheme. But that evening the song upset me. I rebelled against the resignation it implied. Why does God always act too late? Why didn't he get rid of the Angel of Death before he even committed the first murder?

Had our guest stayed with us, he is the one who would have asked these questions. In his absence, I took them up on my own.

The ceremony was coming to an end, and we did not dare look at one another. Father raised his glass one last time and we repeated after him: "Next year in Jerusalem." None of us could know that this was our last Passover meal as a family.

I saw our guest again a few weeks later. The first convoy was leaving the ghetto; he was in it. He seemed more at ease than his companions, as if he had already taken this route a thousand times. Men, women, and children, all of them carrying bundles on their backs, blankets, valises. He alone was empty-handed.

Today I know what I did not know then: at the end of a long trip that was to last four days and three nights he got out in a small railway station, near a peaceful little town, somewhere in Silesia, where his fiery chariot was waiting to carry him up to the heavens: is that not proof enough that he was the prophet Elijah?

5.

Yom Kippur: The Day
Without Forgiveness

With a lifeless look, a painful smile on his face, while digging a hole in the ground, Pinhas moved his lips in silence. He appeared to be arguing with someone within himself and, judging from his expression, seemed close to admitting defeat.

I had never seen him so downhearted. I knew that his body would not hold out much longer. His strength was already abandoning him, his movements were becoming more heavy, more chaotic. No doubt he knew it too. But death figured only rarely in our conversations. We preferred to deny its presence, to reduce it, as in the past, to a simple allusion, something abstract, inoffensive, a word like any other.

"What are you thinking about? What's wrong?"

Pinhas lowered his head, as if to conceal his embarrassment, or his sadness, or both, and let a long time go by before he answered, in a voice scarcely audible: "Tomorrow is Yom Kippur."

Then I too felt depressed. My first Yom Kippur in the camp. Perhaps my last. The day of judgment, of atonement. Tomorrow the heavenly tribunal would sit and pass sentence: "And like unto a flock, the creatures of this world shall pass before thee." Once upon a time—last year—the approach of this day of tears, of penitence and fear, had made me tremble. Tomorrow, we would present ourselves before God, who sees everything and who knows everything, and we would say: "Father, have pity on your children." Would I be capable of praying with fervor again? Pinhas shook himself abruptly. His glance plunged into mine.

"Tomorrow is the Day of Atonement and I have just made a decision: I am not going to fast. Do you hear? I am not going to fast."

I asked for no explanation. I knew he was going to die and suddenly I was afraid that by way of justification he might declare: "It is simple, I have decided not to comply with the law anymore and not to fast because in the eyes of man and of God I am already dead, and the dead can disobey the commandments of the Torah." I lowered my head and made believe I was not thinking about anything but the earth I was digging up under a sky more dark than the earth itself.

We belonged to the same Kommando. We always managed to work side by side. Our age difference did not stop him from treating me like a friend. He must have been past forty. I was fifteen. Before the war, he had been *Rosh-Yeshiva,* director of a rabbinical school somewhere in Galicia. Often, to outwit our hunger or to forget our reasons for despair, we would study a page of the Talmud from memory. I relived my childhood by forcing myself not to think about those who were gone. If one of my arguments pleased Pinhas, if I quoted a commentary without distorting its meaning, he would smile at me and say: "I should have liked to have you among my disciples."

And I would answer: "But I am your disciple, where we are matters little."

That was false, the place was of capital importance. According to the law of the camp I was his equal; I used the familiar form when I addressed him. Any other form of address was inconceivable.

"Do you hear?" Pinhas shouted defiantly. "I will not fast."

"I understand. You are right. One must not fast. Not at Auschwitz. Here we live outside time, outside sin. Yom Kippur does not apply to Auschwitz."

Ever since Rosh Hashana, the New Year, the question had been bitterly debated all over camp. Fasting meant a quicker death. Here everybody fasted all year round. Every day was Yom Kippur. And the book of life and death was no longer in God's hands, but in the hands of the executioner. The words *mi yichye umi yamut*, "who shall live and who shall die," had a terrible real meaning here, an immediate bearing. And all the prayers in the world could not alter the *Gzar-din*, the inexorable movement of fate. Here, in order to live, one had to eat, not pray.

"You are right, Pinhas," I said, forcing myself to withstand his gaze. "You *must* eat tomorrow. You've been here longer than I have, longer than many of us. You need your strength. You have to save your strength, watch over it, protect it. You should not go beyond your limits. Or tempt misfortune. That would be a sin."

Me, his disciple? I gave him lessons, I gave him advice, as if I were his elder, his guide.

"That is not it," said Pinhas, getting irritated. "I could hold out for one day without food. It would not be the first time."

"Then what is it?"

"A decision. Until now, I've accepted everything. Without bitterness, without reservation. I have told myself: 'God knows what he is doing.' I have submitted to his will. Now I have had enough, I have reached my limit. If he knows what he is doing, then it is serious; and it is not any less serious if he does not. Therefore, I have decided to tell him: 'It is enough.' "

I said nothing. How could I argue with him? I was going through the same crisis. Every day I was moving a little further away from the God of my childhood. He had become a stranger to me; sometimes, I even thought he was my enemy.

The appearance of Edek put an end to our conversation. He was our master, our king. The Kapo. This young Pole with rosy cheeks, with the movements of a wild animal, enjoyed catching his slaves by surprise and making them shout with fear. Still an adolescent, he enjoyed possessing such power over so many adults. We dreaded his changeable moods, his sudden fits of anger: without unclenching his teeth, his eyes half-closed, he would beat his victims long after they had lost consciousness and had ceased to moan.

"Well?" he said, planting himself in front of us, his arms folded. "Taking a little nap? Talking over old times? You think you are at a resort? Or in the synagogue?"

A cruel flame lit his blue eyes, but it went out just as quickly. An aborted rage. We began to shovel furiously, not thinking about anything but the ground which opened up menacingly before us. Edek insulted us a few more times and then walked off.

Pinhas did not feel like talking anymore, neither did I. For him the die had been cast. The break with God appeared complete.

Meanwhile, the pit under our legs was becoming wider and deeper. Soon our heads would hardly be visible above the ground. I had the weird sensation that I was digging a grave. For whom? For Pinhas? For myself? Perhaps for our memories.

On my return to camp, I found it plunged in feverish anticipation: they were preparing to welcome the holiest and longest day of the year. My barracks neighbors, a father and son, were talking in low voices. One was saying: "Let us hope the roll-call does not last too long." The other added: "Let us hope that the soup is distributed before the sun sets, otherwise we will not have the right to touch it."

Their prayers were answered. The roll-call unfolded without incident, without delay, without public hanging. The section-chief hurriedly distributed the soup; I hurriedly gulped it down. I ran to wash, to purify myself. By the time the day was drawing to a close, I was ready.

Some days before, on the eve of Rosh Hashana, all the Jews in camp—Kapos included—had congregated at the square where roll was taken, and we had implored the God of Abraham, Isaac, and Jacob to end our humiliation, to change sides, to break his pact with the enemy. In unison we had said *Kaddish* for the dead and for the living as well. Officers and soldiers, machine guns in hand, had stood by, amused spectators, on the other side of the barbed wire.

Now, we did not go back there for *Kol Nidre*. We were afraid of a selection: in preceding years, the Day of Atonement had been turned into a day of mourning. Yom Kippur had become *Tisha b'Av*, the day the Temple was destroyed.

Thus, each barracks housed its own synagogue. It was more prudent. I was sorry, because Pinhas was in another block.

A Hungarian rabbi officiated as our cantor. His voice stirred my memories and evoked that legend according to

which, on the night of Yom Kippur, the dead rise from
their graves and come to pray with the living. I thought:
"Then it is true; that is what really happens. The legend
is confirmed at Auschwitz."

For weeks, several learned Jews had gathered every
night in our block to transcribe from memory—by
hand, on toilet paper—the prayers for the High Holy
Days. Each cantor received a copy. Ours read in a loud
voice and we repeated each verse after him. The *Kol
Nidre,* which releases us from all vows made under con-
straint, now seemed to me anachronistic, absurd, even
though it had been composed in similar circumstances, in
Spain, right near the Inquisition stakes. Once a year the
converts would assemble and cry out to God: "Know this,
all that we have said is unsaid, all that we have done is
undone." *Kol Nidre?* A sad joke. Here and now we no
longer had any secret vows to make or to deny: everything was clear, irrevocable.

Then came the *Vidui,* the great confession. There
again, everything rang false, none of it concerned us anymore. *Ashamnu,* we have sinned. *Bagadnu,* we have betrayed. *Gazalnu,* we have stolen. What? Us? *We* have
sinned? Against whom? by doing what? *We* have betrayed? Whom? Undoubtedly this was the first time since
God judged his creation that victims beat their breasts
accusing themselves of the crimes of their executioners.

Why did we take responsibility for sins and offenses
which not one of us could ever have had the desire or the
possibility of committing? Perhaps we felt guilty despite
everything. Things were simpler that way. It was better
to believe our punishments had meaning, that we had
deserved them; to believe in a cruel but just God was
better than not to believe at all. It was in order not to
provoke an open war between God and his people that
we had chosen to spare him, and we cried out: "You are
our God, blessed be your name. You smite us without
pity, you shed our blood, we give thanks to you for it, O

Eternal One, for you are determined to show us that you are just and that your name is justice!"

I admit having joined my voice to the others and implored the heavens to grant me mercy and forgiveness. At variance with everything my lips were saying, I indicted myself only to turn everything into derision, into farce. At any moment I expected the Master of the universe to strike me dumb and to say: "That is enough—you have gone too far." And I like to think I would have replied: "You, also, blessed be your name, you also."

Our services were dispersed by the camp bell. The section-chiefs began to yell: "Okay, go to sleep! If God hasn't heard you, it's because he is incapable of hearing."

The next day, at work, Pinhas joined another group. I thought: "He wants to eat without being embarrassed by my presence." A day later, he returned. His face even more pale, even more gaunt than before. Death was gnawing at him. I caught myself thinking: "He will die because he did not observe Yom Kippur."

We dug for several hours without looking at each other. From far off, the shouting of the Kapo reached us. He walked around hitting people relentlessly.

Toward the end of the afternoon, Pinhas spoke to me: "I have a confession to make."

I shuddered, but went on digging. A strange, almost child-like smile appeared on his lips when he spoke again: "You know, I fasted."

I remained motionless. My stupor amused him.

"Yes, I fasted. Like the others. But not for the same reasons. Not out of obedience, but out of defiance. Before the war, you see, some Jews rebelled against the divine will by going to restaurants on the Day of Atonement; here, it is by observing the fast that we can make our indignation heard. Yes, my disciple and teacher, know that I fasted. Not for love of God, but against God."

He left me a few weeks later, victim of the first selection.

He shook my hand: "I would have liked to die some other way and elsewhere. I had always hoped to make of my death, as of my life, an act of faith. It is a pity. God prevents me from realizing my dream. He no longer likes dreams."

Nonetheless, he asked me to say *Kaddish* for him after his death, which, according to his calculations, would take place three days after his departure from camp.

"But why?" I asked, "since you are no longer a believer?"

He took the tone he always used when he explained a passage in the Talmud to me: "You do not see the heart of the matter. Here and now, the only way to accuse him is by praising him."

And he went, laughing, to his death.

6.

An Old Acquaintance

In a bus, one summer evening, in Tel Aviv. The sultriness of the day, instead of lessening, leaves behind a heavy stagnant heat which insinuates itself into every pore, weighs on every gesture and breath, blurs every image. People doze on their feet, about to drop into the void. Breathing, even looking, requires immense effort.

We are hardly moving. As we make our way up the principal thoroughfare, Allenby Boulevard, toward the center of town, traffic moves slower and slower and soon it will come to a standstill. Used to this kind of adversity, the passengers demonstrate their wisdom. Some read the

newspaper, others chat or scan the advertisements for
wines, shaving creams, cigarettes. The driver whistles the
latest hit tune. Too bad, I will have to get off at the next
stop. I have an appointment. I shall make it faster on
foot.

But it is a long way to the next stop. We do not seem to
be moving. One bottleneck after another. As if three lanes
of cars had broken down. I want to get off: the doors do
not open until the bus comes to a complete stop. Useless
to argue: the driver's nerves are up to anything. Not
mine. Irritated, I curse myself for not having foreseen
this. I made a mistake to take the bus. And to think we
are in the land of the prophets!

To pass the time I play my favorite game. I pick someone at random and, without his knowing it, establish a
mute exchange. Seated across from me is a middle-aged
man with a lost look. I examine him thoroughly from
head to toe. Easy to classify. Office worker, government
clerk, foreman. The anonymous type. Avoiding extremes,
responsibilities. He takes orders only to transmit them.
Neat, punctual, efficient. He is not at the top of the ladder
nor is he at the bottom. Neither rich nor poor, happy or
unhappy. He just makes a living. He holds his own.
Against everybody.

I put myself in his place: I think and dream like him. I
am the one his wife will greet with love or rancor; the
one who will drown my resentment in sleep or in solitary
drinking; the one my friends betray and my subordinates
detest; the one who has wasted my life and now it is too
late to begin again.

Caught up in the game, I suddenly realize the passenger looks familiar. I have seen before that bald head, that
hard chin, that thin nose. I have seen before that wrinkled forehead, those drooping ears. He turns around to
glance outside, I see his neck: red, naked, enormous. I
have seen that neck before. A shudder runs through me.
It is no longer a matter of curiosity or game. The time

changes pace, country. The present is in the grip of all the years black and buried. Now I am glad I accepted the engagement for this evening, and that I decided against going by taxi.

The passenger does not suspect a thing. He has just lost his anonymity, returned to his prison, but he does not know it yet. Now that I have him, I will not let him get away again. What is he thinking about? Probably nothing. Thinking frightens him. Talking frightens him. Memories, words frighten him: that can be read on his lifeless face. This passenger, I am trying to place him, I know him; I used to practice that same defense myself. The best way to keep from attracting the executioner's attention was not to see him. In order not to be noticed, you must murder imagination: dissolve, blend into the frightened mass, reduce yourself to an object. Go under in order to survive. But the man still does not realize my growing interest in him. Were a hundred of us looking him over, he would not notice any the more.

I leave my seat and stand up directly in front of him. I brush up against him, my knees touch his, but his eyes keep their distance. In a very low voice I say: "I think I know you."

He does not hear. He is playing deaf, blind, dead. Just the way I used to do. He is taking refuge in absence, but tenaciously I track him. I repeat my sentence. Slowly, warily, he comes to life. He raises his tired eyes toward me.

"Were you speaking to me?"

"To you."

"You were saying?"

"I think I have met you somewhere before."

He shrugs his shoulders. "You're mistaken, I don't know you."

The bus starts up, then stops again. I lean over the passenger, who is pretending to ignore me, as if the incident were closed. I admire him: he acts well, he does not even blink. We are so close to one another that our breaths mingle, a drop of my sweat falls onto his shirt. He still does not react. If I were to slap him, he would say nothing. A matter of habit, of discipline. The lesson: conceal pain, because it excites the executioner much more than it appeases him. With me, this technique will not be of any help to him: I know the routine.

"You're not from around here," I say.

"Leave me alone."

"You're from somewhere else. From Europe."

"You're disturbing me. I'd appreciate it if you would stop pestering me."

"But you interest me."

"Too bad. You don't interest me at all. I haven't the slightest desire to talk or listen to you. Go back to your seat before I get angry. You hear me? Beat it!"

The tone of his voice startles me. For an instant, our glances meet. Nothing more is needed: I see myself twenty years ago, a tin plate in my hand, before this all-powerful master who was distributing the evening soup to a pack of starved corpses. My humiliation gives way to a somber joy which I can scarcely contain. According to the Talmud, only the mountains never meet: for the men who climb them, no circle is closed, no experience unique, no loss of memory definitive.

"I have some questions to ask you," I say.

"I don't give a damn about you or your questions."

"Where were you during the war?"

"That's none of your business."

"In Europe—right?"

"Leave me alone."

"In an occupied country, right?"

"Stop annoying me."

"In Germany perhaps?"

The bus stops at last at a station and the man takes advantage of the opportunity: he leaps up and rushes toward the exit; I follow him.

"How odd, we're getting off at the same place."

He steps back quickly to let me pass. "I made a mistake, my stop is further on."

I too pretend to step down and immediately turn back. "How odd, so is mine."

We remain standing near the door. Two women have already taken our places.

"May I go on with our conversation?"

"I don't know who you are or what you could want of me," he says, his teeth clenched. "Your questions are uncalled for, your manners disagreeable and out of place. I don't know what game you're playing, but I refuse any part of it. You do not amuse me."

"You don't remember me. It is understandable. I've changed, I've grown up, I've gained weight, I'm better dressed, I feel well, I walk without fear of collapsing, I lack neither food nor friendship. What about you? How do you feel? Answer me, it interests me. Well, what do you say? No insomnia at night, no pangs of anxiety in the morning?"

Once again he takes shelter behind a mask of indifference, a state of non-being. He thinks himself secure, unattackable. But I pursue him relentlessly:

"Let's start again, shall we? We've established your place of residence during the war: somewhere in Germany. Where, exactly? In a camp. Naturally. With other Jews. You are Jewish, aren't you?"

He answers me with lips so thin they are almost nonexistent, in a tone which still has lost nothing of its assurance:

"Go to hell, I tell you. Shut up. There's a limit to my patience. I would not like to cause a scene, but if you force me . . ."

I pay no attention to his threat. I know he will do nothing, he will not complain, he will not use his fists, not he, not here, not in public: he is more afraid than I of the police. So I proceed:

"What camp were you in? Come on, help me, it's important. Let's see: Buchenwald? No, Maidanek? No, not there either. Bergen-Belsen? Treblinka? Ponar? No, no. Auschwitz? Yes? Yes, Auschwitz. More precisely, in a camp which was part of Auschwitz, Javischowitz? Gleivitz? Monovitz? Yes, that's it—there we are—Monovitz-Buna. Or am I mistaken?"

He performs well, he knows his lesson thoroughly. Not a shiver, not the slightest reaction. As if I weren't speaking to him, as if my questions were addressed to someone else, dead a long time. Still, his efforts not to betray himself are becoming visible now. He controls his hands poorly, clasping and unclasping them; clenching his fingers which he hides behind his back.

"Let's get down to specifics. What did you do there? You weren't just a simple inmate? Not you. You are one of those who knew neither hunger nor weariness nor sickness. You are not one of those who lived in expectation of death, hoping it would not be too long in coming so that they could still die like men and not like unwanted beasts—unwanted even by death itself. Not you, you were head of a barracks, you had jurisdiction over the life and death of hundreds of human beings who never dared watch as you ate the dishes prepared specially for you. It was a sin, a crime of high treason, to catch you unawares during one of your meals. And what about now? Tell me, do you eat well? With appetite?"

He moistens his lips with his tongue. An almost imperceptible sigh escapes him. He has to redouble his efforts not to answer, not to take up the challenge. His muscles stiffen, he will not hold out much longer. The trap is closing on him, he is beginning to understand that.

"What about the barracks number? The seat of your kingdom? Do you remember it? Fifty-seven. Barracks fifty-seven. It was right in the center of the camp, two steps away from the gallows. I've a good memory, haven't I? And you? Is your memory still alive? Or did it bury us all a second time?"

The conductor announces a stop; the barracks-chief does not move: it seems all the same to him. The door opens, a couple gets off, a young mother gets on pushing her little boy in front of her. The driver calls out, "Hey, lady, you owe me a *groosh* or a smile!" She gives him both. We start off again. My prisoner no longer notices: he has lost touch with reality. Outside is the city, so close, so unreal, the city with its lights and its sounds, its joys, its laughter, its hates, its furies, its futile intrigues; outside is freedom, forgetfulness if not forgiveness. At the next stop the prisoner could take flight. He will not, I am sure. He prefers to let me act, decide for him. I know what he is feeling: a mixture of fear, resignation, and also relief. He too has returned to the world of barbed wire: as in the past, he prefers anything whatsoever to the unknown. Here, in the bus, he knows what places him in jeopardy and that reassures him: he knows my face, my voice. To provoke a break would be to choose a danger the nature of which escapes him. In the camp, we settled into a situation this way and for as long as possible did anything to keep from changing it. We dreaded disturbances, surprises. Thus, with me, the accused knows where he stands: I speak to him without hate, almost without anger. In the street, the throng might not be so understanding. The country is bursting with former deportees who refuse to reason.

"Look at me. Do you remember me?"

He does not answer. Impassive, unyielding, he continues to look into the emptiness above the heads of the passengers, but I know his eyes and mine are seeing the same emaciated, exhausted bodies, the same lighted yard, the same scaffold.

"I was in your barracks. I used to tremble before you. You were the ally of evil, of hunger, of cruelty. I used to curse you."

He still does not flinch. The law of the camp: make yourself invisible behind your own death mask. I whisper: "My father was also in your barracks. But he didn't curse you."

Outside, the traffic starts to move, the driver picks up speed. Soon he will shout, "Last stop, everybody off!" I have passed my stop, no matter. The appointment no longer seems important. What am I going to do with my prisoner? Hand him over to the police? "Collaboration" is a crime punishable by law. Let someone else finish the interrogation. I shall appear as a witness for the prosecution. I have already attended several trials of this kind: a former Kapo, a former member of the *Judenrat*, a former ghetto policeman—all accused of having survived by choosing cowardice.

PROSECUTION: "You have rejected your people, betrayed your brothers, given aid to the enemy."

DEFENSE: "We didn't know, we couldn't foresee what would happen. We thought we were doing the right thing, especially at the beginning; we hoped to alleviate the suffering of the community, especially during the first weeks. But then it was too late, we no longer had a choice, we couldn't simply go back and declare ourselves victim among victims."

PROSECUTION: "In the Ghetto of Krilov, the Germans named a certain Ephraim to the post of president of the Jewish council. One day they demanded he submit a list of thirty persons for slave labor. He presented it to them with the same name written thirty times: his own. But you, to save your skin, you sold your soul."

DEFENSE: "Neither was worth very much. In the end, suffering shrinks them and obliterates them, not together but separately: there is a split on every level. Body and mind, heart and soul, take different directions; in this way, people die a dozen deaths even before resigning themselves or accepting a bargain with the devil, which is also a way of dying. I beg of you, therefore: do not judge the dead."

PROSECUTION: "You are forgetting the others, the innocent, those who refused the bargain. Not to condemn the cowards is to wrong those whom they abandoned and sometimes sacrificed."

DEFENSE: "To judge without understanding is a power, not a virtue. You must understand that the accused, more alone and therefore more unhappy than the others, are also victims; more than the others, they need your indulgence, your generosity."

I often left the courtroom depressed, disheartened, wavering between pity and shame. The prosecutor told the truth, so did the defense. Whether for the prosecution or for the defense, all witnesses were right. The verdict sounded just and yet a flagrant injustice emerged from these confused and painful trials; one had the impression that no one had told the truth, that the truth lay somewhere else—with the dead. And who knows if the truth did not die with them. I often used to think: "Luckily, I am witness and not judge: I would condemn myself." Now I have become judge. Without wanting it, without expecting it. That is the trap: I am at the point where I cannot go back. I must pass sentence. From now on, whatever my attitude may be, it will have the weight of a verdict.

The smell of the sea rises to my nostrils, I hear the whisper of the waves, we are leaving the center of the city and its lights. We are coming to the end of the line. I must hurry and make a decision, try my former barracks-chief. I will take on all the roles: first, the witnesses, then the judge, then the attorney for the defense. Will the prisoner play only one role, the accused—the victim? Full powers will be conferred upon me, my sentence will be without appeal. Facing the accused, I will be God.

Let us begin at the beginning. With the customary questions. Last name, first name, occupation, age, address. The accused does not recognize the legitimacy of this procedure, or of the court; he refuses to take part in the trial. It is noted. His crimes are what interest us, not

his identity. Let us open the dossier, examine the charges
leveled against him. Once again I see the scene of the
crime, the uniform face of suffering; I hear the sound of
the whip on emaciated bodies. At night, surrounded by
his sturdy protégés, the accused shows he is skilled in
doing two things at once: with one hand he distributes
the soup, with the other he beats the inmates to impose
silence. Whether the tears and moaning touch him or irri-
tate him does not matter. He hits harder to make them
stop. The sight of the sick enrages him: he senses in them
a bad omen for himself. He is particularly cruel with the
aged: "Why are you hanging on to this disgusting, filthy
life? Hurry up and die, you won't suffer anymore! Give
your bread to the young, at least do one good deed before
you croak!"

One day he saw my father and me near the barracks.
As he always did, my father was handing me his half-full
bowl and ordering me to eat. "I'm not hungry anymore,"
he explained and I knew he was lying. I refused: "Me
neither, Father, really, I'm not hungry anymore." I was
lying and he knew it, too. This same discussion went on
day after day. This time the barracks-chief came over and
turned to my father: "This your son?"—Yes.—"And you
aren't ashamed to take away his soup?"—But . . . —"Shut
up! Give him back that bowl or I'll teach you a lesson you
won't soon forget!"

To keep him from carrying out that threat, I grabbed
the bowl and started eating. At first I wanted to vomit but
soon I felt an immense well-being spread through my
limbs. I ate slowly to make this pleasure, stronger than
my shame, last longer. Finally, the barracks-chief moved
on. I hated him, and yet, down deep, I was glad that he
had intervened. My father murmured, "He's a good man,
charitable." He was lying, and I lied too: "Yes, Father,
charitable."

How do you plead: guilty or not guilty?

My father did not conceal his pride: his son had

obeyed him. As in the past. Even better than in the past.
So there was, in the camp, in the midst of this organized
insanity, someone who depended on him and in whose
eyes he was not a servile rag. He did not realize that it
had not been his will I had been performing, but yours. I
was aware of that, and so were you, but I refused to think
of it; you did not. I also knew that by obeying you both as
your slave and your accomplice, I was cutting short my
father's life by one breath, by one awakening. I buried
my remorse in the yellowish soup. But you were wiser
and certainly shrewder than my father; you were not deceived. As you moved away, you had an air of assurance,
as if to say: "That's the way it is, that's life, the boy will
learn, he'll find his way and who knows? someday maybe
he'll succeed me." And I did not give the soup back to my
father. I did not hurl myself at you and tear from you
your eyes and your tongue and your victory. Yes, I was
afraid, I was a coward. And hunger was gnawing at me:
that's what you had counted on. And you won.

Has the accused anything to say in his defense?

You always won, and sometimes, at night, I thought
that maybe you were the one who was right. For us, you
were not just the whip or the ax in the murderer's hand:
you were the prince who played the game of death, you
were its prophet, its spokesman. You alone knew how to
interpret the rages of the executioner, the silences of the
earth; you were the guide to follow; whoever imitated
you, lived; the others would perish. Your truth was the
only valid truth, the only truth possible, the only truth
that conformed to the wishes and designs of the gods.

Guilty or not guilty?

Instead of rejoining the ranks of the victims, of suffering like us and with us, instead of weeping without tears
and trembling before the incandescent clouds, instead of
dying like us and with us, perhaps even for us, you chose
to reign over the work of darkness, proclaiming to
whomever wanted to hear that pity was criminal, gener-

osity fruitless, senseless, inhumane. One day after the roll-call you gave us a long lecture on the philosophy of the concentration camp: every man for himself, every man the enemy of the next man, for each lived at the other's expense. And you concluded: "What I am telling you is true and immutable. For know that God has descended from heaven and decided to make himself visible: I am God."

How do you plead?

The judge hears the stifled moans of the witnesses, living and dead; he sees the accused beat up one old man who was too slow in taking off his cap, and another because he did not like his face. "You, you look healthy to me," says the accused, and punches him in the stomach. "And you, you look sick to me, you're pale," and he slaps his face. Itzik has a heavy shirt: the accused takes it away from him. Itzik protests and he is already writhing in pain. Izso has held onto his old shoes: the accused claims them. Izso, clever, hands them over without saying a word. The accused takes them with a contemptuous smile: look at this imbecile, he does not even resist, he does not deserve to live.

Well, then? Guilty or not guilty?

And what if everything could be done over again? What are you now compared to what you were then? Tell us about your repentance, your expiation. What do you tell your wife when she offers you her pride, when she speaks of the future of your children? What do you see in the eyes of the passerby who says to you "good morning," "good evening," and *"shalom,"* "peace be with you"?

"Well?" yells the driver. "How many times do I have to tell you we're here?"

He looks at us in his rear-view mirror, shouts louder. Our inertia is too much for him. He turns around in his seat and shouts again: "Boy, you must be deaf! Don't you understand Hebrew?"

My prisoner pretends not to understand any language.

He sleeps, he dreams, transported somewhere else, in another time, the end of another line. He is waiting for me to make the first move, to break the curse that separates us from other men. As in the past with his masters, he will follow, he will obey.

The driver is getting angry. These two speechless and immobile phantoms apparently want to spend the night in his bus. Do they think they are in a hotel? He gets up, grumbling, "I'll show you, you'll see." He moves toward us, looking furious. My prisoner waits for him without flinching, indifferent to whatever may happen. I touch his arm.

"Come on, let's go."

He complies mechanically. Once down, he stands stationary, and wisely waits for me on the sidewalk. He could make a dash for the dark little streets that lead to the ocean. He does not. His will has defaulted. He is not about to upset the order of things, to speculate on an uncertain future. Above all, no initiative, that was the golden rule at camp.

The bus starts up and leaves: here we are alone. I have nothing more to say to him. A vague feeling of embarrassment comes over me, as if I had just done something foolish. All of a sudden, I become timid again. And in a weak voice I ask him: "You really don't remember me?"

In the darkness I can no longer make out his face. I no longer recognize him. Doubt chokes me: and what if it was not he?

"No," he says, after a long silence, "I don't remember you."

I no longer recognize the sound of his voice. It used to be gruff, cutting. It has become clear, humane.

"And yourself? Do you remember who you were?"

"That is my business."

"No. It is my business, too."

I suddenly think I must put an end to this: but how? If he whimpers and justifies himself and begs my forgive-

ness, I will have him arrested. And if he keeps on denying
everything? What would he have to say for me to let him
go? I do not know. It is up to him to know.

Abruptly he stiffens. I know his eyes have regained
their coldness, their hardness. He is going to speak. At
last. In defending himself he is going to throw all the
light on this mystery to which we remain chained forever.
I know he will speak without altering the thin line of his
lips. At last he is speaking. No: he is shouting. No! he is
yelling! Without preparation, without warning. He insults me, he is offensive. Not in Hebrew—in German. We
are no longer in Israel but somewhere in the universe of
hate. He is the barracks-chief who, his hands clasped behind his back, "advises" one of his slaves to leave at once
or he will regret the day he was born. Will he hit me,
break my bones, make me eat dirt, as he is threatening to
do? No one would come to my aid: in camp it is the
strongest and most brutal who is in the right. Is he going
to crush me in his claws, murder me? If he does, I will
carry his secret with me. Can one die in Auschwitz, after
Auschwitz?

The barracks-chief is lecturing me the way he used to
and I do not hear what he is saying. His voice engulfs me,
I let myself drown in it. I am no longer afraid. Not of
dying nor even of killing. It is something else, something
worse. I am suddenly aware of my impotence, of my defeat. I know I am going to let him go free, but I will never
know if I am doing this out of courage or out of cowardice. I will never know if, face to face with the executioner, I behaved like a judge or a victim. But I will have
acquired the certitude that the man who measures himself against the reality of evil always emerges beaten and
humiliated. If someday I encounter the Angel of Death
himself in my path, I will not kill him, I will not torture
him. On the contrary. I will speak to him politely, as
humanely as possible. I will try to understand him, to
divine his evil; even at the risk of being contaminated.

The barracks-chief is shouting obscenities and threats; I do not listen. I stare at him one last time without managing to distinguish his features in the night. My hands in my pockets, I turn around and begin to walk, slowly at first, then faster and faster, until I am running. Is he following me?

He let me go. He granted me freedom.

7.
The Promise

Once upon a time there was a poor visionary who set out to rescue the damned from the darkness in which they dwelt. So that they might be compelled to live, he proclaimed himself immortal.

I cannot remember his name, nor how old he was: perhaps I never knew. I remember only his face and, above all, the eyes which dominated it. He had the face of a madman and the eyes of a saint, as though two persons were at war within him. When he spoke, his lips barely moved and his voice seemed to come from a long way off. It was the voice of a man who challenges mountains.

The place where I met him was dark, as though some

magician had plunged it into eternal night. It was peo-
pled with phantoms. There were countless thousands of
them. They had no past and no future. They were outside
of time, beyond history. They were building a one-way
Jacob's Ladder, gigantic and invisible, which they were
all waiting to climb, so that the heavens might be purified
by fire. Man was leaving the earth, recalled by God.
Everything was to start again. Creation had failed. The
age-old vision had degenerated into a curse.

But my visionary friend refused to believe all that. He
claimed that we were in the Holy of Holies, in the presence of the Messiah. What he lacked in humor he made
up in imagination.

He was one of the Righteous; we called him "the
Prophet." Affectionately, meaning to tease and provoke
him. I do not know who first called him by that name, nor
why. Nor do I know whether it pleased or irritated him.
All I know is that it suited him. The Prophet talked like a
prophet. Making us relive our past, he gave us back our
homes and our memories. And yet, as we listened in silence, with lumps in our throats, it was always of the
future that he spoke. The truth was that we needed a
future.

There was something reassuring and comforting in his
presence, tall, gaunt, and emaciated. We thought, if he,
with his ravaged body, can endure so much, so can we.
He worked like all the others, and, like all the others, he
suffered cold and hunger and the brutality of the guards.
I never heard him complain. His cheerfulness and vitality
amazed us. What was the source of his strength and his
faith? We had no idea.

We had no idea, either, where he came from, or what
he had done before the war. We were staggered by what
he knew, the number of countries he had seen, the many
languages he spoke.

He could have been a Pole, a Belgian or an Austrian.

He could have been a doctor or a philosopher, a rabbi or a poet, a beggar or a gardener. Every group felt that he belonged to them. When asked, he would evade the question with a smile. "My past wouldn't interest you. What matters is my future."

Well, if he chose to be secretive, we forgave him. We loved him too well to hold it against him. His secrets and his weaknesses were no concern of ours. It was what he was doing now, frankly and openly, that concerned us and won our gratitude: his persistent endeavors to make our lives bearable. We loved him because he responded to every appeal for help, he set his face against evil, he clung to his humanity in a world where humanity was denied—and he took very little credit for it.

He wanted no thanks. He would say:

"All that I do is done in your name. I am only your representative." Or, "It is you who have made me what I am; it is I who owe you a debt of gratitude." We loved him because he wanted to restore our self-respect, to make us think better of ourselves when we thought of him, who was so different from us. And when, as sometimes happened, he was withdrawn and silent, we respected his reserve. His private thoughts were nobody's business but his own.

Until the day when, transformed, he announced his decision to reveal himself to a world that had ceased to expect his coming.

It was a Saturday in autumn, a Saturday red with blood. We were clearing up rubble in a factory which had been bombed the night before. Foaming at the mouth with rage, the masters took it out on their slaves. Pointing to the rubble, the officer in charge of the working party warned us: "You'd better not start gloating too soon. Whoever wins this war, it won't be *you*." The guards, to prove it to us there and then, launched into a ferocious attack. They laid about them indiscriminately. There were three dead and nine injured in our party alone.

Morale had never been so low. The struggle, it seemed to us, was futile. We would not be there to celebrate the defeat of Germany. Worn out, with heavy hearts, we felt that the end was near. We had touched rock bottom.

But not the Prophet. Blows could not crush him. Maimed as he was, he walked with firm step, head held high and resolution in his eyes. Tirelessly he went from one to another of us, imploring us to stick it out, not to lose hope. In vain. We had not the strength to listen to him.

At night, after the roll-call, he would make us sit on our bunks while he stood and preached endurance. "Brothers, fellow Jews, listen to me. I only ask that you should hear me out. We have no right to go under. If we are not there to bear witness on our own behalf, who will do it for us? Where, after the long night, should the first ray of light come from, if not from us? The day will come when everything will have to be told, and if we do not tell what we know, no one will.

"Who, if not ourselves, will raise the hue and cry after the mad murderers? For the day is at hand, deliverance is in sight. You have my word for it, my promise. For God's sake, my friends, don't give up. Hold fast to me! I give you the future! Do not reject it! Hold fast, I say!"

For the first time, his appeal fell on deaf ears. "What's the meaning of this?" he thundered angrily. "Don't you trust me? Have you ever known me to lie to you?"

Somebody tried to calm him. "You must forgive us. We're not to blame any more than you are. We can't take any more." Another added: "You offer us the future, but the Germans have already put an end to that." A third said: "Oh! yes, Prophet, that's the way it is. The Germans' prophecy has beaten yours!"

The Prophet lowered his head, and was silent. I could not help feeling sorry for him. Was he going to surrender, and fall into line with the rest? It seemed so. He was defeated. He would never try to rally us again. I thought: we have betrayed him.

After what seemed an endless silence, he jerked himself upright. He was no longer the same man. He was convulsed, trembling with fury. Panting, his face contorted, he threw his feverish glance over his audience, who, looking vague, were only waiting for him to leave before relapsing into torpor.

We longed for nothing better, in our apathy, than the void of oblivion. Our only hope was that we should soon be hurled over the precipice. No more thinking, no more planning, no more hopeless dreams. We wanted to be done with them, and the stifling and oppressive anguish they caused us. We longed to drown in the muddy waters of a river that would never reach the sea, to die while our bodies still lived.

"You won't even try to understand!" suddenly thundered the preacher. No response. We were incapable of understanding. We were impatient to see him gone. And besides, what was there to understand? I thought: this teller of tales has no more tales to tell.

It seemed that I was right. He moved toward the door with an impatient gesture. But he never took his eyes off us, and stopped after every step, sure that, in spite of everything, we would call him back.

Were we not his friends, his brothers? No. Dumbly, we watched him go, and no one called him back. But he came back: "You won't even try to understand," he repeated, but this time sounding hurt rather than angry. "Very well, then, I shall have to compel you. You leave me no choice."

There was no longer any trace of anger in his voice. It was once again the sad, beautifully modulated voice of the prophet of hope.

With his hands clasped behind his back, he paced the floor, and revealed his private vision to us all:

"When misfortune strikes some of the people of Israel,

all the people are stricken at the same time. All the sufferings of our people are rungs on the ladder of history. The enemy who persecutes us doesn't single out our merchants, our sages, our fools, or our poets. He who kills a Jew aims to kill all the Jews. Bankers and rabbis, vagabonds and dreamers, old men and children, we are sores on the body of Israel.

"This is true also of the Messiah. You relegate him to the heavens, but he is here among us. You imagine that he is safe, sheltered from danger, but he has come here to be with the victims. Yes, even he, he better than anyone, knows the sorrows that consume you; he feels the fist that smashes into your faces. The darkness that engulfs us engulfs him also. It is he, here and now, who urges you not to give way to despair. It is he who has need of you. Do not abandon him. Take pity on him. He is worthy of your pity. You must make sure that he is not the only one among his people to survive."

To strengthen his argument, he quoted from the sayings and legends of the Talmud:

"It is written that when mankind has wholly given way to good or evil, the Messiah will appear. Well, mankind has given way to evil, and we know it. No one can claim to be free from guilt. We are living proof that man has betrayed his nature and his destiny. It is our duty to proclaim the end of his reign. Without our knowledge, it has already been proclaimed.

"We are the harbingers of a new era. Very soon the *shofar* will sound, and the pall of darkness will be lifted. If you stand firm for a day, a week, a month, you will witness the coming of the dawn, and men will kneel to you and ask forgiveness. It is I who make you this promise, it is he who has decreed it."

Oh, yes, he spoke well. As always. His words came fast and fiery. But we remained deaf to their poetry. His message turned to dust and ashes before it could touch us.

"I am not surprised that you do not believe me," he

concluded, half-sadly, half-teasingly. "But you heard me out. That will have to do for the present. Besides, I am now going to reveal a truth which even you will not deny. Do you know why you call me the Prophet? Because that is what I am."

That night, in my dreams, I heard him laughing and crying, though I could not guess the reason.

Needless to say, we did not take what he said seriously. Yet we took him seriously. Whether he was playing a part no one could tell, but if so, he was determined to play it to the bitter end. While playing his chosen part, he somehow managed to involve us. Whether as spectators or participants, we could not escape watching him at work.

In all he did, he gave of himself unstintingly, caring for the sick, willingly bearing the burdens of hard labor and torture, sharing his bread with anyone who asked for it. He lived only for others. He was admired by some and pitied by others. At his approach, people would stop talking. They would exchange winks, and whisper that the poor soul was going out of his mind.

His friends, growing more and more uneasy, urged him to take a grip on himself, to stop squandering his energies. It was a sin, they said, to tempt providence so recklessly. He shrugged, and went back to work with redoubled zeal. Far from avoiding excess, he deliberately sought it.

I asked him, "Why do you take such risks?"

He replied, "I have nothing to lose."

"Have you no fear of death?"

"Why should I fear it?"

"But what are you trying to prove?"

"That I am not a liar."

He seemed to bear a charmed life. It was fascinating. How long could his luck hold? People made bets on it, and it was always the doubters who lost. The Prophet was proving indestructible.

On one occasion he came up against Hans the Killer, the most dreaded of all the Kapos in the camp. Hans claimed that a jar of jam had been stolen from him. He stormed into our hut and, with threats and insults, demanded that the culprit be denounced, or else we should all pay for it.

The Prophet stepped forward: "It is I."

Taken by surprise, Hans stared in bewilderment.

Unflinching, the Prophet reiterated: "I am the thief."

The Killer, collecting himself, roared: "And the jam? Where is it?"

"I ate it," calmly answered the Prophet.

For a long time, the two men looked at each other in silence. Hans was frowning. A bad sign. I held my breath and shut my eyes, but only for an instant. I opened them again, to see a Hans transformed. The notorious killer was doubled up with laughter: "You're lying! I made it up. The jam? In the cupboard! Come with me, I'll show you." And he made him a present of his life, and of a large hunk of bread.

We no longer knew what to think.

Soon after this, the winter selection took place. It was the Prophet's last, and fatal, trial. The camp doctor pronounced him unfit for work. The whole camp was shocked at the news, and it was decided that something must be done to save him.

An emergency committee was formed. There was only a week left to rescue him. A week in which to raise funds, make representations to influential people, bribe guards, work out a plan of action. There was solidarity on a scale unprecedented in the camp. More than a hundred people were involved. Never had so much been done by so many prisoners, and all to save a single Jew.

Why him? Because everyone loved him. There was not

one of us whom he had not helped at some time. Everyone owed him a debt of gratitude. Moreover, we felt obscurely that he symbolized our ability to rise above circumstances. It seemed to us that our own survival depended upon his. We still did not believe that he had the gift of prophecy, but we acted as though he were the arbiter of our destiny.

He, for his part, made light of the matter. Did he know of our tremendous efforts to rescue him? Yes. And it amused him. He realized before we did, better than we did, that our efforts were doomed to failure. There was no appeal from the death sentence.

Just a week after the selection, on a bright winter morning, the Prophet was ordered to stay in the hut. He was excused from work that day. We knew what that meant. So did he. His friends' eyes were full of tears, but not his. Up to the last minute he was still playing his chosen part, still offering consolation and encouragement.

He smiled as he took leave of us. "There is no need for tears. Take your choice: either I am myself or I am he. In either case, one thing is certain: he will not abandon you. So what is there to weep for?"

He left us. We never saw him again. I still know nothing about him. Who was he? Where did he come from? I know only where he went.

I often think of him, especially when I hear the Hasidic chant, *Ani Maamin,* which proclaims the faith of the Jew and the coming of the Messiah. As a child, I believed fervently. I still believe, but now chiefly in the hope that faith will restore the old fervor.

In any event, the promise made by the Prophet on the night of his "revelation" was kept: we, all of us who were with him, survived.

8.

Testament of a Jew from Saragossa

One day the great Rebbe Israel Baal Shem-Tov ordered his faithful coachman to harness the horses as fast as he could and drive him to the other side of the mountain.

"Hurry, my good Alexei, I have an appointment."

They came to a stop in a dense forest. The holy man stepped down, went over to lean against an oak, meditated for a moment, then climbed back into the carriage.

"Let's go, Alexei," he said, smiling. "We can go back now."

Though accustomed to not understanding the behavior of his master, the miracle-worker, the coachman still had the courage to be astonished.

"But your appointment? Did you miss it? You, who always arrive on time, who never disappoint anyone? Did we come for nothing?"

"Oh no, my good Alexei, we did not come so long a way for nothing. I have kept my appointment."

And as happened whenever he banished a bit of misery from the world, the Rebbe's face radiated happiness.

According to Hasidic tradition it is not given to man to measure the extension of his actions or the impact of his prayers, no more than it is given the traveler to foresee his precise destination: that is one of the secrets of the notion of *Tikkun*—restoration—which dominates Kabbalism.

The wanderer who, to purify his love or to free himself from it, travels around the world and does not know that everywhere he is expected. Each of his encounters, each of his stops, without his knowing, is somewhere inscribed, and he is not free to choose the paths leading him there.

Souls dead and forgotten return to earth to beg their share of grace, of eternity; they need the living to lift them out of nothingness. One gesture would suffice, one tear, a single spark. For each being participates in the renewed mystery of creation; each man possesses, at least once in his life, the absolute power of the *Tzadik*, the irrevocable privilege of the just to restore equilibrium, to repair the fault, to act upon the absent. Condemned to go beyond himself continually, man succeeds without being aware of it and does not understand until afterward.

And now let me tell you a story.

Traveling through Spain for the first time, I had the strange impression of being in a country I already knew. The sun and the sky, the tormented lustre in the eyes: landscapes and faces familiar, seen before.

The strollers on the *ramblas* in Barcelona, the passersby and their children in the back streets of Toledo:

how to distinguish which of them had Jewish blood, which descended from the Marranos? At any moment I expected Shmuel Hanagid to appear suddenly on some richly covered portico, or Ibn Ezra, Don Itzchak Abarbanel, Yehuda Halevi—those princes and poets of legend who created and sang the golden age of my people. They had long visited my reading and insinuated themselves into my dreams.

The period of the Inquisition had exercised a particular appeal to my imagination. I found fascinating those enigmatic priests who, in the name of love and for the sacred glory of a young Jew from Galilee, had tortured and subjected to slow death those who preferred the Father to the Son. I envied their victims. For them, the choice was posed in such simple terms: God or the stake, abjuration or exile.

Many chose exile, but I never condemned the Marranos, those unhappy converts who, secretly and in the face of danger, remained loyal to the faith of their ancestors. I admired them. For their weakness, for their defiance. To depart with the community would have been easier; to break all ties, more convenient. By deciding to stand their ground on two levels simultaneously, they lived on the razor's edge, in the abnegation of each instant.

I did not know it when I arrived in Spain, but someone was awaiting me there.

It was at Saragossa.

Like a good tourist, I was attentively exploring the cathedral when a man approached me and, in French, offered to serve as guide. Why? Why not? He liked foreigners. His price? None. He was not offering his services for money. Only for the pleasure of having his town admired. He spoke of Saragossa enthusiastically. And eloquently. He commented on everything: history, architecture, customs. Then, over a glass of wine, he transferred his amiability to my person: where did I come from, where was I going, was I married, and did I believe in God. I replied: I come from far, the road before me will be long. I eluded his other questions. He did not insist.

"So, you travel a great deal," he said politely.

"Yes, a great deal."

"Too much, perhaps?"

"Perhaps."

"What does it gain you?"

"Memories, friends."

"That's all? Why not look for those at home?"

"For the pleasure of returning, no doubt, with a few words I didn't know before in my luggage."

"Which?"

"I can't answer that. Not yet. I have no luggage yet."

We clinked glasses. I was hoping he would change the subject, but he returned to it.

"You must know many languages, yes?"

"Too many," I said.

I enumerated them for him: Yiddish, German, Hungarian, French, English, and Hebrew.

"Hebrew?" he asked, pricking up his ears. *"Hebreo?* It exists?"

"It does exist," I said with a laugh.

"Difficult language, eh?"

"Not for Jews."

"Ah, I see, excuse me. You're a Jew."

"They do exist," I said with a laugh.

Certain of having blundered, he looked for a way out. Embarrassed, he thought a minute before going on: "How is Hebrew written? Like Arabic?"

"Like Arabic. From right to left."

An idea seemed to cross his mind, but he hesitated to share it with me. I encouraged him: "Any more questions? Don't be shy."

He said: "May I ask a favor of you? A great favor?"

"Of course," I said.

"Come—come with me."

This was unexpected.

"With you?" I protested. "Where to? To do what?"

"Come. It will take only a few minutes. It may be of importance to me. Please, I beg you, come."

There was such insistence in his voice that I could not say no. Besides, my curiosity had gotten the upper hand. I knew that Saragossa occupied an important place in Jewish history. It was there that the mystic Abraham Aboulafia was born and grew up, the man who had conceived the plan to convert to Judaism Pope Nicholas III himself. In this town, anything could happen.

I followed my guide home. His apartment, on the third floor, consisted of only two tiny rooms, poorly furnished. A kerosene lamp lit up a portrait of the Virgin. A crucifix hung opposite. The Spaniard invited me to sit down.

"Excuse me, I'll only be a second."

He disappeared into the other room and returned again after a few minutes. He was holding a fragment of yellowed parchment, which he handed me.

"Is this in Hebrew? Look at it."

I took the parchment and opened it. I was immediately overwhelmed by emotion, my eyes clouded. My fingers were touching a sacred relic, fragment of a testament written centuries before.

"Yes," I said, in a choked voice. "It is in Hebrew."

I could not keep my hand from trembling. The Spaniard noticed this.

"Read it," he ordered.

With considerable effort I succeeded in deciphering the characters, blurred by the passage of some four hundred years: "I, Moses, son of Abraham, forced to break all ties with my people and my faith, leave these lines to the children of my children and to theirs, in order that on the day when Israel will be able to walk again, its head high under the sun, without fear and without remorse, they will know where their roots lie. Written at Saragossa, this ninth day of the month of *Av,* in the year of punishment and exile."

"Aloud," cried the Spaniard, impatient. "Read it aloud."

I had to clear my throat: "Yes, it's a document. A very old document. Let me buy it from you."

"No," he said sharply.

"I'll give you a good price."

"Stop insisting, the answer is no."

"I am sorry."

"This object is not for sale, I tell you!"

I did not understand his behavior.

"Don't be angry, I did not mean to enrage you. It's just that for me this parchment has historical and religious value; for me it is more than a souvenir, it is more like a sign, a . . ."

"For me, too!" he shouted.

I still did not understand. Why had he hardened so suddenly?

"For you too? In what way?"

He explained briefly: it was the tradition in his family to transmit this object from father to son. It was looked upon as an amulet the disappearance of which would call down a curse.

"I understand," I whispered, "yes, I understand."

History had just closed the circle. It had taken four centuries for the message of Moses, son of Abraham, to reach its destination. I must have had an odd look on my face.

"What's going on?" the Spaniard wanted to know. "You say nothing, you conceal your thoughts from me, you offend me. Well, say something! Just because I won't sell you the amulet you don't have the right to be angry with me, do you?"

Crimson with indignation, with anxiety perhaps, he suddenly looked evil, sinister. Two furrows wrinkled his forehead. Then it was he who was awaiting me here. I was the bearer of his *Tikkun,* his restoration, and he was not aware of it. I wondered how to disclose it to him. At last, finding no better way, I looked him straight in the eye and said: "Nothing is going on, nothing. I am not angry with you. Know only this: you are a Jew."

And I repeated the last words: "Yes, you are a Jew. *Judeo.* You."

He turned pale. He was at a loss for words. He was choking, had to hold himself not to seize me by the throat and throw me out. *Judeo* is an insult, the word evokes the devil. Offended, the Spaniard was going to teach me a lesson for having wounded his honor. Then his anger gave way to amazement. He looked at me as if he were seeing me for the first time, as if I belonged to another century, to a tribe with an unknown language. He was waiting for me to tell him that it was not true, that I was joking, but I remained silent. Everything had been said. A long time ago. Whatever was to follow would only be commentary. With difficulty, my host finally regained control of himself and leaned over to me.

"Speak," he said.

Slowly, stressing every syllable, every word, I began reading the document in Hebrew, then translating it for him. He winced at each of the sentences as though they were so many burns.

"That's all?" he asked when I had finished.

"That's all."

He squinted, opened his mouth as if gasping for air. For an instant I was afraid he would faint. But he composed himself, threw his head back to see, on the wall behind me, the frozen pain of the Virgin. Then he turned toward me again.

"No," he said resolutely. "That is not all. Continue."

"I have given you a complete translation of the parchment. I have not left out a single word."

"Go on, go on, I say. Don't stop in the middle. Go on, I'm listening."

I obeyed him. I returned to the past and sketched a

picture of Spain at the end of the fifteenth century, when
Tomas de Torquemada, native of Valladolid, Grand In-
quisitor of gracious Queen Isabella the Catholic, transformed the country into a gigantic stake in order to save
the Jews by burning them, so that the word of Jesus
Christ might be heard and known far and wide, loved and
accepted. Amen.

Soon the Spaniard had tears in his eyes. He had not
known this chapter of his history. He had not known the
Jews had been so intimately linked with the greatness of
his country before they were driven out. For him, Jews
were part of mythology; he had not known "they do
exist."

"Go on," he pleaded, "please go on, don't stop."

I had to go back to the sources: the kingdom of Judea,
the prophets, the wars, the First Temple, the Babylonian
Diaspora, the Second Temple, the sieges of Jerusalem and
Masada, the armed resistance to the Roman occupation,
the exile and then the long wait down through the ages,
the wait for the Messiah, painfully present and painfully
distant; I told him of Auschwitz as well as the renaissance
of Israel. All that my memory contained I shared with
him. And he listened to me without interrupting, except
to say: "More, more." Then I stopped. I had nothing more
to add. As always when I talk too much, I felt ill at ease,
suddenly an intruder. I got up.

"I have to leave now, I'm late."

The car would be waiting for me in front of the cathedral. The Spaniard took me there, his head lowered, listening to his own footsteps. The square was deserted: no
car in sight. I reassured my guide: there was no reason to
worry, the car would not leave without me.

We walked around the building once, twice, and my
guide, as before, told me more about the Cathedral of
Notre-Dame del Pilar. Then, heavy with fatigue, we
found ourselves inside, seated on a bench, and, there, in
that quiet half-darkness where nothing seemed to exist

anymore, he begged me to read him one last time the testament that a Jew of Saragossa had written long ago, thinking of him.

A few years later, passing through Jerusalem, I was on my way to the Knesset, where a particularly stormy debate was raging over Israel's policy toward Germany. At the corner of King George Street, a passerby accosted me:

"Wait a minute."

His rudeness displeased me; I did not know him. What was more, I had neither time nor the inclination to make his acquaintance.

"I beg your pardon," I said. "I'm in a hurry."

He grabbed my arm.

"Don't go," he said in a pressing tone. "Not yet. I must talk to you."

He spoke a halting Hebrew. A tourist, no doubt, or an immigrant recently arrived. A madman perhaps, a visionary or a beggar: the eternal city lacks for none. I tried to break away, but he would not let go.

"I've a question to ask you."

"Go ahead, but quickly."

"Do you remember me?"

Worried about arriving late, I hurriedly replied that he was surely making a mistake and confusing me with someone else.

He pushed me back with a violent gesture.

"You're not ashamed?"

"Not in the least. What do you want? My memory isn't infallible. And judging from what I see neither is yours."

I was just about to leave when under his breath the man pronounced a single word: "Saragossa."

I stood rooted to the ground, incredulous, incapable of any thought, any movement. Him, here? Facing me, with me? I was revolving in a world where hallucination

seemed the rule. I was witnessing, as if from outside, the
meeting of two cities, two timeless eras and, to convince
myself that I was not dreaming, I repeated the same word
over and over again: "Saragossa, Saragossa."

"Come," said the man. "I have something to show you."

That afternoon I thought no longer about the Knesset
or the debate that was to weigh on the political conscience of the country for so long. I followed the Spaniard
home. Here, too, he occupied a modest two-room apartment. But there was nothing on the walls.

"Wait," said my host.

I sank into an armchair while he went into the other
room. He reappeared immediately, holding a picture-
frame containing a fragment of yellowed parchment.

"Look," the man said. "I have learned to read."

We spent the rest of the day together. We drank wine,
we talked. He told me about his friends, his work, his first
impressions of Israel. I told him about my travels, my
discoveries. I said: "I am ashamed to have forgotten."

An indulgent smile lit his face.

"Perhaps you too need an amulet like mine; it will keep
you from forgetting."

"May I buy it from you."

"Impossible, since it's you who gave it to me."

I got up to take leave. It was only when we were about
to say good-bye that my host, shaking my hand, said with
mild amusement: "By the way, I have not told you my
name."

He waited several seconds to enjoy the suspense, while
a warm and mischievous light animated his face:

"My name is Moshe ben Abraham, Moses, son of Abraham."

9.
Moshe the Madman

Of all the faces that haunted my childhood, that of Moshe the Madman stands out most clearly in my memory. As if I were his only link to reality and he to mine.

With the passing years, I shall have forgotten certain of my playmates and most of the companions I knew before and during the war. Not him. As if we were one another's prisoners. Wherever I go, he precedes me. Sometimes I no longer know which of us pursues the other.

Yet I know he has been dead for a very long time; in reality, his death coincided with that of my childhood. But he refuses to admit it. He seems to abuse the privileges of death and fire to deny the facts.

The facts are irrefutable: twice condemned, as Jew and mental defective with no means of support, he was part of the first transport to leave the ghetto. First stop: the old synagogue. Moshe took advantage of it to lead the prayers. He laughed. It was the greatest day of his life: never could he have imagined that he would pray in this famous place, before a congregation of three thousand. Second stop: the railway station. Moshe was singing and dancing, perhaps to revive everybody else's courage, perhaps simply because he had never taken a train before. Third and last stop: the platform of another forsaken little station no longer in use. Walking at the head of a silent procession, Moshe was still singing, louder and louder, until the end, as if to mock an enemy known only to himself.

That enemy did not succeed in silencing his deep, disturbing voice. That voice wanders through the world, as dangerous to hear as not to hear. Often, during the night, it draws me out of my sleep. I experience once again the fear of a child afraid to sleep alone. I sense his presence there, in the room, in the corner near the mirror or in front of the window overlooking the river. Huddled up, I remain awake till morning; I wait for the early morning noises of the city to reach me before I dare to move.

In the past I approached him without fear. He came often to our house. Father was his friend, his confidant. I had been warned: "Be kind to him, he's mad." I did not know the meaning of the word. He himself was to say to me: "Take a good look at me, I'm mad." I looked but did not understand. To people he used to meet ten times in the same day, he would introduce himself the same way every time: "You don't know me, I'm Moshe the Madman." "We know, we know," they would say as they pushed him out of their way. "No, not enough, you'll never know it enough."

He fascinated me. People regarded him with pity, yet he dominated them. He was everywhere the center, the oracle; he moved in another universe, and it was only through him that we could become a part of it. We divined a power in him capable of crushing us.

The disturbing fixity of his gaze gave him a sly mean look; yet with me he was kind, friendly. I would gladly interrupt my reading to go and listen to his heartbreaking songs. He told me strange stories, too, without endings. "Only the beginning interests me," he used to say. "Who cares about the end, I know what it will be." "And what about the beginning?" I asked. "I know that, too, except that I'm trying to change it."

To interrupt the study of Talmud was not really a sin if it meant spending an hour with him. He knew more about the Talmud than the sages of two thousand years ago and their disciples. He saw further than they, his silences contained a truth more hidden than theirs. Perhaps he perceived in it the first madman that God created and whom he himself must have resembled. He derived from that great compendium not facts and affirmations but vision and inspiration. He was the first to make me understand that I could and must think of myself as a stranger; and that I must—and could—kill that stranger, or else be destroyed by him.

Rather than reject his madness, Moshe evoked it. It served him as refuge, as homeland, and when on a rare occasion I visit an asylum, I experience in the presence of each patient, the same respectful fear that Moshe inspired in me long ago. The prophet winking at me: it is he. The persecuted one, who spurns me: him again. The young woman serenely rocking an invisible infant: it is Moshe she is trying to calm. All of them have his look.

I am apt to pass him on the street as well. And to have him at my side in a restaurant or theater, to sit next to him in a plane. Sometimes I think the entire universe is inhabited by but a single person, that all faces are fused into one. Suddenly the young lady with whom I am strolling appears stupid; the words which I drink in ring hollow; friendships become burdensome. I want to run away, but Moshe guards all the exits. Armed with unknown power, he commands and I obey: it is my life against his. To escape him, I would have to destroy him. But how does one assassinate an angel gone mad?

One day I thought I had found the solution: I imprisoned him in a novel. With a roof over his head, an address, a home, surrounded by people who showed him affection, I thought he would at last leave me in peace. It was not until later, the work finished, that I noticed the trick he had played on me: without my knowledge, like a thief, he had insinuated himself into the other characters (without respect to age, sex, or religion). In turn it was he who said, "I," "you," "he." Two people were speaking to one another: he was both at once. They tormented one another: he was the cause and the expression of their suffering. Panic-stricken, I reread my earlier narratives: there too, he reigned as master. There too, he had preceded me. Even more serious: he had accorded himself the status of temporary resident, turning up and disappearing as he pleased. Hardly was he unmasked than he was already running off, more savage than ever, to new adventures to which he was dragging me by force.

The idea occurs to me at times that I myself am nothing but an error, a misunderstanding: I believe I am living my own life, when in fact I am only transmitting his.

One morning a stranger telephoned. He was speaking Yiddish and his drawling, melodious accent betrayed his Hungarian origin. I was struck by his voice, which seemed familiar.

"To whom am I speaking?" I inquired politely.

If ashamed of his own name, he did not take the trouble to make up another. Instead, he had the skill of losing himself in generalities.

"My name? Why do you ask? You don't know me. Besides, it's of no importance. What is in a name? A convention, a decoy. Tell me, what is more deceptive than a name? Even God has none, you know."

"He can permit himself that liberty," I said, half-amused, half-irritated. "No one is likely to confuse him with anyone else."

"You don't know a thing about it. Besides, who told you that that could not apply just as well to me? After all, I was created in his image, was I not?"

I had heard this voice before, harsh, disturbed, disturbing: but where? when? under what circumstances? Could it belong to a forgotten friend? a friend returned to life? an old neighbor with an account to settle with me?

"Do I know you?"

"You amaze me: does anyone ever really know anyone?"

I lost patience.

"We're wasting time, sir. What exactly do you want?"

"I told you: to meet you."

"For what purpose?"

"Oh, none in particular. I'd like to see you, talk to you, understand you."

"You amaze me," I replied. "Does anyone ever really understand anyone?"

"You refuse? You don't have the right."

He deigned to explain himself: he was what one might call an admirer. He claimed to have read certain of my works. He wanted to discuss a certain aspect which concerned him personally.

I hardly enjoy playing the sage in direct communication with heaven. I do not live in the castle, the prince does not confide in me.

"Then you refuse?" my reader insisted. "You don't want to meet me, simply because my name means nothing to you?"

I had heard that voice before, that accent.

"Give me an hour. I absolutely must see you. It's about your town. I think I recognize it."

I had not been mistaken. He came from a small town in my region. He remembered my native town, which he used to visit several times a year. He also remembered Moshe the Madman, who on two occasions had been engaged as the official cantor for the High Holy Days in the only synagogue in his village. I jumped: Moshe the Madman? Well then, that changed everything.

"Really?" I shouted, excitedly. "You knew him? You heard him sing? When? How was he, what mood was he in? Did you speak to him? What did he say to you? When was the last time you saw him?"

"You're asking too many questions. We can't talk over the telephone. It's about him I wanted to question you. But your time is precious. Too bad. I'm sorry."

"Wait! I didn't say that!"

"I thought that . . ."

"Forget what I told you."

Now I was the one insisting that we meet. When? As soon as possible. Right now? He was not free. This afternoon? Too busy. This evening? Already taken. He was playing hard to get: he could not see me before next week. I pleaded, he let himself be convinced: just to please me, he would free himself the next day. After his work, at seven. I invited him to my place. Too far: he lived in Brooklyn. For want of a better place, we agreed to meet at the public library on Forty-second Street. At the main entrance. All right? All right. To make doubly sure, I offered to describe myself. Unnecessary, he said.

He hung up, laughing, and his laugh, even more than his voice, seemed familiar.

And so I learned that in this stone-faced city someone else had kept alive the memory of that cantor who used to play the supreme fool, then the fallen fool, in order to provoke the heavens and to entertain the children.

Who could he be? An old man retracing his steps one

last time before condemning himself for good? His son, in search of the past, of old wounds? An orphan who wanted to understand? Tomorrow I would know. For the moment, the waiting was enough. I already felt less alone: my memory was no longer going to be a prison enclosing other prisons each more narrow and more suffocating than the last. The doors were going to open from the outside. At last I would have some corroboration that Moshe the Madman had really and truly existed, that he had not just forced his way into my imagination.

I needed very much this tangible evidence, this testimony. For as a result of responding to his call, of hearing his breath, I had come to doubt his existence: I believed it a reflection if not an extension of my own. He had accompanied me so often and so far that I was ending up by confusing our destinies, our thrusts; I sang like him, I prayed like him, like him I tried to probe the silences of others, to oppose them with my own. I was he.

It was thus with a feeling approaching gratitude that I thought of my unknown friend from Brooklyn: thanks to him, I would become myself again. Provided that nothing happened to him, that he did not die first, that he did not lose his memory....

Later, on my way home from work, a certain uneasiness suddenly comes over me: what if the Hungarian Jew from Brooklyn is not a stranger? I have to stop in the middle of the street and rest against the wall of a skyscraper. I review our conversation, which seems stranger now than it did that morning: why had he refused to give his name? to come to my house? Why had he waited until the last moment to mention the cantor's name? And what had made him laugh? I am conscious of an obscure danger. If he is not a stranger, who is he? What does he want of me?

I shake myself and start walking again. It is getting late, I am exhausted. I follow the river. Not a soul in sight. Yet, I keep stopping at every corner to look back:

am I being followed? I hold my breath: nothing. Just
nerves. A car comes, its headlights blind me, I jump back.
It has passed. Who is driving it? Don't think about anything. At last, my building. The porter opens the door for
me and looks quizzically at me. He thinks I am drunk, I'm
with someone. I go up to the twenty-fourth floor. My
room. I am afraid to turn on the light. Groping, I move
toward the bed, I undress in the dark. I feel I am being
watched. To sleep. To hide myself in sleep. A thousand
hands reach toward me and summon me: I am afraid, but
I let them carry me away, I want to give myself up to that
voice, to understand why it sounded so familiar; I am
afraid, but I want to understand why I am afraid . . . and
so round and round until I fall asleep.

An hour before the rendezvous, I stationed myself at
the entrance to the library. The department stores were
pouring their shoppers out into the street, where wave
after wave of them flooded the sidewalks. Pedestrians and
drivers were engaged in their daily battle. There was no
end to the congestion. The heat gave the passersby a dull
look of resignation. Men and women, young and old,
walked hand in hand. Some out of habit, others so as not
to get lost. The crowd was getting larger by the minute.

Standing motionless, to one side, I scrutinized those
sweating faces: would I recognize the one I was waiting
for?

At precisely seven, a man came up and stared right at
me. He had not recognized me. But I did recognize him.
Those smoldering eyes, those puffy lips, that stooped
back. The rest hardly mattered. His appearance did not
count. In the past, he had been dressed only in rags. Now
he appeared elegant in his light gray suit, with matching
tie. In the past, he used to play the beggar; now he was
playing the rich man.

"Moshe," I murmured in a choked voice.

He held out his hand.

"Hello. Glad to meet you. How are you?"

His voice was grave, melodious. His gesture hesitant. And his expression disturbing, supplicating and mocking at the same time.

I could not believe my eyes. My head was bursting. He was holding my hand in his and I did not have the strength to withdraw it. I thought: "You've got to think, and fast." But I did not dare to think: who knew where my thoughts would lead me? If Moshe the Madman is alive, then all those who disappeared, lost in the mist, are alive, too; something has happened in the kingdom of night which we know nothing about, something quite different from what we think.

He let go my hand and stared at me curiously, as if to test me.

"You called me Moshe: why?"

"Oh, I don't know. Inadvertently, out of habit. It's a name I like, it contains the history of our people."

It was he, my friend, the mad cantor, who was staring at me, no doubt about it. I had seen him go to his death and that was still the best proof he was alive: all those who entered, by night, the crucible of death, emerged from it by day more healthy and more pure than the others who had not followed them.

Suddenly I understood why he had haunted me since the liberation: I saw him everywhere because he was everywhere, in every eye, in every mirror. The dead had come back to earth, all like him; he was the first link in this dynasty of madmen, he was destiny turned into man.

He no longer had his pot-belly or his thick beard. He no longer wore his prayer-shawl, his *talit katan*, under his patched-up jacket. But it was the same Moshe who used to shout in the street, in front of the synagogue, at the hour of prayer: "I am burning, children, I am burning like fire! Look, children, look and see that it is in every-one's power to burn without being consumed!" People thought he was drunk. He liked to drink. During the holidays he would go to various Hasidic groups, and interrupting their gatherings, would jump up on the table and in a single draught empty every bottle handed him. He was the king of clowns, the prophetic fool, free to do anything. The more he drank, the more his utterances gained in clairvoyance. "Yes, I'm burning, children!" he would cry. "Look at me and understand that it is with fire that one kindles fire, it is also with fire that one puts out the flame: but woe to the man who puts it out, woe to him who draws back from it. Look, children, look and see how I hurl myself down head first!"

"Let's go and have something," my companion suggested.

We found a kosher restaurant on Forty-sixth Street. The waiter placed a bottle of Slivovitz on the table. We clinked glasses. I said: "Moshe used to drink alone. I should have kept him company, but I was too young. Is it too late now? I wonder."

I filled the glasses a second time. A third. I emptied mine in one draught; he was nursing his, taking small sips. I thought: "He has changed, after all. In the past, he would have been impatient, he would have wanted to rush things. Is it possible that he has reached the end of his road?"

"I read what you wrote about Moshe the Madman," he said, grimacing slightly. "You seem to know him better than I."

"Better? Perhaps differently."

"No, better. The proof: you speak of him, he animates your writings. That's why I was determined to meet you. What do you know about him? his background? his ambitions? his secret plans? Are you sure he was the way you describe him? that he didn't use his madness to achieve an end known only to himself? And then, are you sure he was killed at Auschwitz?"

I would have wanted to interrupt: "You've misunderstood me, I've expressed myself badly, I wrote badly and you misread me. Now I know the truth, and the truth is that Moshe the Madman isn't dead nor will he ever die, just as his vision will never be extinguished." But I said nothing and let his phrases rain down on me like a punishment I deserved.

At last, when I could stand no more, I cried: "What do you want from me? What have I done to you? Who gives you the right to judge me, to accuse me? Moshe the Madman? He didn't condemn anyone, but you do. In the name of what? of whom?"

He placed his hand on mine to calm me.

"You're getting carried away, don't be angry. I've offended you: I beg your pardon."

I thought: "Yes, indeed, he has changed after all. Moshe never begged anyone's pardon, not even God's, especially not God's."

He took a swallow and continued, his voice a little lower: "I was so curious that I let myself take advantage of your kindness, do you understand?"

"Let's not talk about it anymore. Let's drink up. The best way to evoke the cantor is to drink."

To gain forgiveness, he gulped down the contents of his glass; then, after a moment of hesitation, he continued: "One last question. Perhaps it will offend you. You speak of him lovingly. Always. You speak of him the way I do of my father. Why is that?"

He wanted to tell me the story of his life, his experiences before, during, and after the war. I hardly cared to hear about them. I was becoming confused, I was beginning to lose my temper, my thoughts were getting tangled up, I was losing my way.

"Let's get back to your question. Why do I evoke his memory with love? Because nobody else does. Because he was no one's father, no one's son. Homeless, rootless, job-

less: a free man, so to speak. Nothing outside tempted or
frightened him. Unreliable, solitary, he made of his madness a contagious joy, a public good. A guide, he showed
the way. A visionary, he never drank twice from the same
cup, never invited the same experience twice. How could
I recreate his image without love, his destiny without
longing?"

I could have gone on that way until morning, but I fell
silent. Suddenly the idea came to me that we really knew
nothing about him, except what he himself had forced us
to see. Perhaps he had had a family in a neighboring
village, had loved a woman, brought up children. What
could we say, exactly? That he proclaimed himself a
madman, that he confused happiness and poverty, lucidity and hallucination. But the rest? The side he would
not show? I was beset by doubts. I took another look at
the Jew from Brooklyn.

"The truth," I whispered. "I insist you tell me the truth.
You have information I need. Give it to me. Who are you?
Why does the cantor interest you? Could you be his
brother? his friend? his murderer? his avenger? Could
you be—his son?"

My question seemed to surprise him. He flushed and
began to blink, his eyelids seized with a nervous tic he
made scarcely any attempt to control. After a moment of
silence, he regained possession of himself and burst out
laughing.

"You're joking! You're wandering off! What an imagination you have! Me, his avenger! Me, his son!"

"You laugh, but that proves nothing. You are laughing
to conceal your little game, but I see through it. Tell me
who you are and what you're doing here, in front of me. I
must know everything, I tell you."

He became serious again and began to inspect his fingernails. My eyes clouded over.

"Well? Nothing more to say? Too bad. If Moshe the

Madman were here, he'd know how to conquer you. But he is no longer of this world. Moshe the Madman never was of this world. All the same, I knew him and have followed him to this very day. That must prove something, but I shall die without knowing what."

He was biting his nails, sweat was streaming down his forehead. I frightened him, that was clear. Because I was unmasking him? Or because he had just had a glimpse of the cantor's other face? Or because he took me for Moshe the Madman himself? Sadly, he shook his head a few times, then got up suddenly to announce, in a dazed, staccato voice, that he had to leave.

As if through a fog, I watched him make his way to the door; he stopped in front of the cashier, paid the check, gave the waiter a tip, came back to take one last look at me, then left. I should have held him back, run after him, forced him to admit everything. The cantor would have done that, but I was incapable: I had had too much to drink.

I began to look distractedly at the other customers, who, fortunately, were not concerned about me. Young couples were smiling at each other and forgetting to eat; old people were eating in silence, as if out of spite. Little by little, the restaurant began to empty. In my turn, I got up and left, reeling. I soon found myself in Times Square again, that grim fair where the down-and-out come to unload their desperations. Bathed in neon light, numbed by music from jukeboxes, the lonely passersby drag themselves from one bar to another. I walked aimlessly all night. Then I made my way homeward, along the river, reinvigorated by the freshness of the morning breeze. The effects of the alcohol disappeared, I regained my equilibrium, I began to see clearly. My behavior in the restaurant filled me with shame, I had made a spectacle of myself. After all, the Jew from Brooklyn, whose name I still did not know, was only a curious reader intent on meeting a fellow countryman. The rest had been the work of my sick imagination. He, poor fellow, had nothing to do with it.

Blessed Moshe, I thought, smiling: you've played another trick on me. You will never change.

And yet, I retain a question from this episode which I must add to all the other questions concerning the cantor from my town. Perhaps, in my drunkenness, I had seen clearly after all. Perhaps Moshe the Madman, being no one's son, is the father of us all.

10.

The Wandering Jew

No one knew his name or his age: perhaps he had none. He wanted no part of what ordinarily defines a man, or at least places him. Through his bearing, his knowledge, his way of taking various and contradictory positions, he aspired to embody the unknown, the uncertain: his head in the clouds, he made use of his learning to obscure clarity—no matter what kind, no matter where it came from. He liked to move fixed points, to destroy what seemed secure. He reproached God for having invented the universe.

Where did he come from? What were his joys, his

fears? What did he seek to attain, to forget? Nobody
knew. At some point in his life, had he known women,
happiness, disappointment? A mystery seven times
sealed. He spoke of himself only to throw people off: yes
and no had the same value, good and evil pulled in the
same direction. Using similar tactics, he constructed and
demolished his theories at a single blow. The more one
listened, the less one learned about his life, about the
world within him. He possessed the superhuman power
of remaking the past for himself.

He inspired fear. Admiration, too, of course. People
used to say: "A dangerous character—he knows too many
things." Talk like that pleased him. He wanted to be
alone, strange, inaccessible.

He popped up almost everywhere, always unexpect-
edly, only to disappear a week later, a year later, without
leaving any trace. He would turn up, always by chance,
on the other side of a frontier, a mountain: as miracle-
working rabbi, businessman, servile beadle. He had been
around the world several times without money, without
passport; no one will ever know how or to what end.
Perhaps he had done it precisely so that no one would
ever know.

His birthplace was, now Marrakech, now Vilna, then
Kishinev, Safed, Calcutta, or Florence. He produced so
many proofs, so many details that he managed to be con-
vincing about each place as the final verity. But the next
day the edifice would crumble: he would describe, in
passing, the enchanting atmosphere of his native town,
somewhere in China or Tibet. The vastness of his exag-
gerations exceeded the level of falsehood: it was a philosophy.

The outcome of his real or imaginary voyages? He
talked much and well. He had mastered some thirty ancient and modern languages, including Hindi and Hungarian. His French was pure, his English perfect, and his
Yiddish harmonized with the accent of whatever person

he was speaking with. The *Vedas* and the *Zohar* he could recite by heart. A wandering Jew, he felt at home in every culture.

Always dirty, hairy, he looked like a hobo turned clown, or a clown playing hobo. He wore a tiny hat, always the same, on top of his immense round bloated head; his glasses, with their thick, dirty lenses, blurred his vision. Anyone encountering him in the street without knowing him would step out of his way with distaste. To his own great satisfaction, moreover.

For three years, in Paris, I was his disciple. At his side I learned a great deal about the dangers of language and reason, about the ecstasies of sage and madman, about the mysterious progress of a thought down through the centuries and of a hesitation through a multitude of thoughts. But nothing about the secret which consumed or protected him against a diseased humanity.

Our first meeting was brief and stormy. It took place in a small synagogue, on the Rue Pavé, where I often went on Friday nights to take part in the services welcoming the Sabbath.

After prayers, the faithful gathered around an old man, repulsive in appearance, who, with flamboyant gestures, began to explain the *Sedra*—the biblical passage—for that week. His voice sounded harsh, disagreeable. His delivery was rapid, his phrases ran into one another, he was difficult to follow, and this was intentional: it amused him to confuse his audience. We understood each word, each idea, and yet we had the impression that we were being deluded, that the old man was making fun of all who claimed to understand. But no one resisted: to let oneself be taken in became one of the mind's pleasures—an unhealthy one.

Suddenly, in the middle of a sentence, he saw me. He interrupted himself.

"Who are you?"
I told him my name.
"Foreigner?"
"Yes."
"Refugee?"
"Yes."
"Where from?"
"Oh," I said, "from far away. From over there."
"Religious?"
I did not answer. He repeated: "Religious?"
I still did not answer.
He said: "Ah, I understand."
And he went on with his questioning without giving
my embarrassment a thought.
"Student?"
"Yes."
"Of what?"
"I'd like to study philosophy."
"Why?"
I remained silent.
But he insisted: "Why?"
"I'm searching."
"What are you searching for?"
I was going to correct him: "whom," not "what." But I
got hold of myself and answered: "I don't know yet."
He was not convinced.
"What are you looking for?"
I said: "For an answer."
His voice was cutting: "An answer to what?"
I was going to correct him: "to whom," not "to what."
But I looked for the simplest way out: "To my questions."
He let out a spiteful little laugh.
"Ah," he said, "you have questions, you?"
"Yes, I do have some."
He held out his hand.
"Give them to me; I'll give them back to you."
I looked at him, confused. I did not understand.

"I will," he said, "I'll give them back to you with all the answers."

"What?" I cried. "You have answers to questions? And you expect to be able to state them publicly?"

"Of course," he replied. "If you want proof, I can provide it on the spot."

I was silent a moment and said: "No, in that case I prefer to take you at your word."

"I don't like that." He was becoming irritable.

"I can't help that," I said, blushing. "But if you can answer my questions, then I no longer have any."

The old man—how old was he, seventy? older?—stared at me for a long time; so did the faithful. Suddenly I was afraid, I felt threatened. Where could I hide?

The old man bent his heavy head forward.

"Ask me a question just the same," he said in a conciliatory tone.

"I told you: I no longer have any."

"Of course you do. Just one. No matter which. You'll see, you won't regret it. You have nothing to fear."

I was not quite convinced. On the contrary, I had everything to dread. The first submission would bring another in its wake. There would be no end to it, no way out.

"Well?" said the old man, friendly now. "Just one question."

My obstinacy made him furrow his brow; a dark flash passed through his eyes.

"This is pure stupidity, my boy. I offer you a short-cut and you reject it: are you sure you have the right? Who told you your coming to France had any other purpose than to meet me?"

My heart was beating fast, I bit my lips. An inner voice put me on guard. I was at a crossroads, I had to be careful, keep my eyes open, remain quiet, avoid taking a road that might not be my own.

"Well? You choose to be stubborn? Have you lost your

tongue? your memory? Or do you think you're strong enough to disobey me?"

He was becoming impatient. My fear grew, I was suffocating. Like a child, I saw a messenger in every stranger: it was up to me alone to receive his promise or his curse. My teachers had taught me never to trust appearances, to suffer a thousand humiliations sooner than inflict a single one. According to the Talmud, to humiliate someone in public is to shed his blood. Refusing to play this old man's game was to attack his honor.

"Have you decided?" he asked, his eyes mean. "Are you finally going to open your mouth?"

With difficulty, prudently, so as to have done with him, I managed to query him about a certain passage in the Bible. Too easy a question for his taste. He demanded another: still too easy. And another. His face tightening, he drove me on.

"Are you making fun of me? Go ahead, throw yourself into it, go to the end, all the way to obscurity, and bring back to me whatever escapes you, whatever baffles you."

After my tenth or twelfth try, he declared himself more or less satisfied. He closed his eyes and went into an explication, the brilliance and rigor of which dazzled me. I was already his, I entrusted him with my will, my reason. He spoke and I could only admire the extent of his knowledge, the richness of his thought. His words wiped out distances, obstacles: there was no longer beginning or end, there was only the voice, harsh and disagreeable, of a man explaining to the creator the mysteries and inadequacies of his creation.

When he finished I said, "That was beautiful."

I had been moved and I would have liked to shake his hand. And tell him: "You trouble me, I will follow you." But his expression suddenly changed and I dared not move. His bloated face grew purple with rage. He approached me, seized me by the shoulders, shook me violently, and began to shout with contempt.

"That's all you can find to say? That it was beautiful?
You imbecile, I scoff at beauty. It's nothing but façade,
it's only decoration: words die away in the night without
enriching it. When will you understand that a beautiful
answer is nothing? Nothing more than illusion? Man defines himself by what disturbs him and not by what reassures him. When will you understand that you are living
and searching in error, because God means movement
and not explanation."

With that he relaxed his attack and hurried out
quickly, leaving behind his heavy and mysterious anger.

Somebody burst out laughing and consoled me.

"Don't let it bother you, young man. He's strange in
his relations with people who admire him or flee him. You
mustn't hold it against him, that would only lead you into
his trap anyway. You mustn't take his insults to heart. He
likes to provoke suffering, it's his favorite pastime, his
stimulant. He has already ridiculed people older than
you, more learned too. He wouldn't be able to survive
without his daily victim."

And so, for the first time, I came up against his legend.
I learned many stories praising his strength; he knew
everything about everybody while always himself remaining in shadow. He had read every work, important or obscure, penetrated every secret, traveled through
every country; he was at home everywhere and nowhere.
Nobody knew where he lived, what he lived on. Who
were his friends, his rivals? People called him Rebbe and
did not even know whether he was observant. He recognized no law, no authority, neither that of the community
nor that of the individual. Did he submit to divine will?
There again, mystery. He seemed to arrive, always unex-
pectedly, from a distant shore, some enchanted country.
The years had no hold over his body, nor over his mind:
he was ageless. He remained the same, defying the imagination, provoking time itself.

Until late in the evening, those Jews in the synagogue

talked to me about him, and I listened, straining painfully, as I had listened long ago, as a child, amazed, to the
stories the Hasidim used to tell with such fervor, between
the prayers of *Minhah* and *Maariv*, stories of the miracles
wrought by the *Tzadik*, the companion and servant of
God.

"Don't let it bother you, young man," repeated the man
who was trying to console me. "It's a privilege to be insulted by our visitor."

"But who is he? What does he do when he doesn't have
a victim in hand? Where does he hide and why? What
must one do to meet him?"

The Jews shrugged their shoulders. Some thought him
fabulously rich, others completely impoverished. "He's a
madman who makes fun at our expense," declared one old
gray-beard. His neighbor protested: "No, no, he is a
saint, one of the just, and his mission on earth is to shake
us up; we all need to have someone stir us up from time
to time, no?" The bearded man assented: "Indeed, you
are right, we do need it, otherwise the soul would rot in
its casing. But I tell you, I don't like our visitor, I don't
trust anyone who doesn't trust me; I think he's in the
service of Satan, it's Satan who protects him and assures
him his victories. To what end, at what price? I'd like to
know. I'm afraid of knowing."

Someone recalled the following episode. During the
occupation, our itinerant orator was arrested by the Germans. When interrogated by a Gestapo officer, he declared he was Alsatian, Aryan, and, what's more, a professor of higher mathematics in a German university. The
officer guffawed:

"You teach at the university? You? You expect me to
swallow that?"

"Certainly," said the vagabond, without blinking.

"Show me your papers."

"I lost them. In a bombing raid."

The officer leaned forward, then said to the accused:

"You've fallen into the wrong hands, my little Yid. In civilian life I myself am a professor of higher mathematics."

The Jew was not the least bit upset.

"What luck, my dear colleague! Happy to make your acquaintance! Naturally, I could propose that you question me. But, I have a better suggestion. I will give *you* a little examination. Here is a problem. If you find the solution, shoot me: I promise not to protest. But if it escapes you, you will let me go without asking any more questions."

The officer accepted the bargain. The "professor" soon found himself free again and then succeeded in crossing into Switzerland, where the Chief Rabbi became one of his devoted admirers. How did he manage to get across the border?

"Nothing could be more logical," said the suspicious old man. "It was Satan who came to his aid."

"Not at all," retorted his neighbor. "Do you really imagine Satan would help a Jew save his skin? I maintain our visitor is blessed—which would explain everything. Death had no hold over David while he was chanting his Psalms; in the same way, it is powerless before our visitor so long as he disturbs our torpor. Like all of us, death stands in awe of his temper."

That night I could not and did not want to sleep. After leaving the synagogue I walked the streets and alleys of the sleeping city, driven on by an unacknowledged hope that I would see him rise before me, behind me, suddenly, like a criminal, like a sage in the guise of a beggar, to tell me: "Dawn is breaking, follow me." Dawn broke, I went home alone.

I had to find him again, no matter at what cost. It was him I had been seeking since the end of the war, since the death of my teachers, since their fire consumed itself among the burning coals, somewhere in Silesia. He alone would be in a position to take their place and show me

what road to follow, and perhaps even reveal where it
leads. To find him again, confront him, beg him. But
where? With whose help? With what clue, with what
help? I returned often to the synagogue on Rue Pavé; the
faithful already knew me and understood the true purpose of my visits: it was not God who drew me there.
They teased me, indulgently: "Hey there, young man,
you want to be insulted some more?" "Yes," I answered.
They smiled: "Patience, young man, patience. He will
return, he always returns, but it is impossible to predict
when, with him it's impossible to predict anything."

Yes, he was the wandering Jew. Was he still in France?
Think him here, he was already elsewhere, always somewhere else, in India, in Morocco, in Katmandu, in the
heat of the desert or sailing the high seas: how was one to
know? With him, all certainties turned to dust.

A few months later. Gare du Nord. I was taking the
train for Taverny. I made my way there twice a week to
teach a class on the prophets to a group of young Polish
and Hungarian refugees, all of them survivors of the
camps; in transit in France, they were living in an O.S.E.
chateau while awaiting visas for Palestine.

My nose in my notes, I was going over my lecture when
someone called out to me. I gave a start: that disagreeable, harsh voice. Yes, it was he. Unshaven, dirty, in rags,
wearing the same old little hat: a circus character.

"Come here!" he shouted at the top of his voice.
"There's a seat here, next to me!"

The passengers shot us disapproving glances. I felt embarrassed and relieved at the same time: embarrassed to
be seen in the company of a creature so ugly, but relieved
to have found him again at last, when I had been sure I
would never see him again.

"Where are you going?"

I told him the purpose of my trip. He gave his irony
free rein.

"No, really? Extraordinary! I'd have expected anything but that! You, a professor, you! Now we've seen everything! The seeker turned guide, that's it, isn't it? Well, good, tell me about it. Tell me what you teach them, your pupils. Let me profit from it, too, won't you?"

I did not want to, but he insisted. Seized with uneasiness, I could oblige only by mumbling some incoherent sentences about the Book of Job: that tale was in high style then, every survivor of the holocaust could have written it. In my class I spoke of the origin of the dialogue between man and his fellowman. And between God and Satan. I also dealt with the importance attributed to silence as a setting. Then the idea of friendship and justice, and to what extent the one diminishes the other. And the notion of victory in prophetic thought. What is man? Ally of God or simply his toy? His triumph or his fall?

Feigning interest, my companion stared at me with a condescending look. He was enjoying himself, that was obvious. He did not interrupt, but periodically emitted dry groans which added to my agitation: I no longer knew what I was saying, nor what I was trying to prove. Everything was muddled in my mind, I was hearing myself talk and it was someone else who was reciting a badly-learned, disjointed lesson. Everything rang false. Finally, I stopped, out of breath, on the verge of tears.

"That's all?" asked the hobo, implacable.

"Yes, I think so . . ."

"Ah well, poor Job," he scoffed, "as if he hadn't already suffered enough without you!"

With that, he subjected me to a close interrogation which was to have been the final blow. My knowledge, acquired over the years at the cost of many sleepless nights and much renunciation, now slipped away like sand. I believed I knew the Talmud? Mistake. I thought I understood Rashi's commentaries? Illusion. I could recite the Psalms by heart? So much the worse; that was pure presumption since I did not even grasp the first line.

The blood was pounding in my temples, a vague pain

was spreading through my body. Then I had lived for
nothing, cheating, lying to myself. I had wasted my childhood, my youth; all my experience was nothing but
empty boast. Like Job, I cursed the day I was born, I
wanted to die, to disappear, to expunge my shame, to
redeem myself. The hobo found this amusing. The more I
talked, the deeper I sank into my own ignorance. I was
touching madness, I was going to lose the use of my
tongue, become a child again, speechless, innocent. I
began to pray: "Please, God, let us reach Taverny soon,
before it is too late, because I can bear it no more." Taverny signified the promised land; there torturer and
victim would say good-bye, or better farewell, my punishment would come to an end. The slowness of the subur-
ban train exasperated me. Ordinarily the trip lasted an
hour, but now it seemed to be taking eternity. Still, the
hobo granted me no respite: his harsh and unpleasant
voice pursued me. I thought: "The gray-bearded old man
at the synagogue was right; he is Satan, he wants to destroy me; I won't put up with him any longer, let him go
away, let him leave me in peace, I won't play his game
anymore."

Suddenly the train stopped. The conductor called out:
"Taverny-y-y!" I shook myself to pull myself together.
Ironically, the hobo imitated my gestures. I held out my
hand: "I get off here." He stood up and said: "So do I."
And he pretended not to understand my confusion.

Below, near the exit, I asked him where he was going.

"What a question! With you, of course!"

"With me?" I cried out, horrified.

"Yes, I've decided to accompany you."

But why? For what reason? He did not know yet.

"I'll know when we get there."

But for the love of heaven, who had invited him? No
one, of course.

"I consider myself a free man, I go where I please,
when I please, with whomever I please."

"And what about me? How do I figure in your calculations?"

"Too soon to tell, we'll see."

After a silent walk of about twenty minutes, we arrived at the chateau, where the sight of my companion provoked general laughter. I was intending to return to Paris the same night. I stayed a whole week. So did he.

My class was to meet outdoors, in the early afternoon. During lunch the old man watched me in silence; he was making me ill. I did not touch the food. Neither did he.

My nerves raw, I discouraged conversation at the table. I had premonitions of disaster: with him here, my exposition was sure to be a failure. How to get him out of the way? Say to him: "I beg you, Mr. Unknown, please be so kind as to go for a walk and come back this evening"? Sooner bury myself alive. Besides, my request would have been in vain. This was too good an opportunity for him, he was not going to miss it.

The director sent his charges outdoors for the lecture. With a heavy heart, I followed my pupils. I knew I was lost, there was nothing more to do: the die had been cast.

My companion sat down at my left. Seated in a semicircle under a huge tree whose branches seemed about to collapse, the students scrutinized us with a mischievous look. The hobo intimidated me, that was clear, and they could hardly understand why. They chattered among themselves and exchanged unkind remarks about him, no doubt about me as well. I called for silence while realizing that I had forgotten everything: I no longer knew even which chapter we were supposed to discuss. Fortunately, at the last moment, just as I was about to open the session, the grotesque old man touched my arm and curtly announced his decision to speak in my place. The pupils roared with laughter. I have never felt so relieved. The speaker cleared his throat.

"I know you are studying the tragedy of Job. I suggest

we leave him to dress his wounds. I have the impression he has been badly mishandled here these past few weeks."

He gave me a side-glance: had I withstood the blow? I lowered my head. My loyal students appreciated the humor of my replacement; they were no longer laughing at him but at me.

"Here's a suggestion," the speaker went on seriously. "Suppose each of you tells me what subject is closest to his heart: then I shall discuss them all in a piece. But one condition: make sure the subjects are all different. I hate repetition."

This rhetorical game became an unforgettable experience. Bible, *Midrash, Zohar:* the questions fused together. Some students, to carry the test to the point of absurdity, questioned him on international politics, on the atomic bomb, and even on superstition in the Middle Ages. The lecturer took no notes whatsoever; his eyelids lowered, closed, he waited until everyone had a turn. Then, without making a move, without preliminary remarks, he attacked the topics head-on, discoursing on each individually and on all together. His voice sounded harsh and unpleasant, but no one took notice. Spellbound, we listened to him, our minds burning, holding our breath, transformed, transported into a strange universe where all beings and objects ripped off their veils, where everything held together and strained toward an Absolute, no matter which, and where—by force of words alone, of nuance, too—man discovered his power and obligation to dispel the chaos which precedes and often follows all creation, to impose on it a meaning, a future. Suddenly each of us realized that all these themes, brought up by chance, pell-mell, were in reality linked to a center, to the same core of clarity. Yes, Cain's act contains within it that of Titus. Yes, the sacrifice of Isaac prefigures the holocaust, the song of David calls to that of Jeremiah: *hafoch ba vehafoch ba dekula ba,* the Torah is

a whole and everything is in the Torah. Why is the first
letter of *Breshit* (the first book of the Pentateuch) *Bet*
and not *Aleph?* Because man is too weak to begin: someone has already begun before him. Jacob had chosen exile
in order to permit Moses to choose liberty. Whoever turns
and looks at the summit of the mountain knows that the
beginning prepares the end and that man can act upon
his creator, who also studies Torah.

In the distance, the village churchbell had long since
sounded midnight, but the speaker, tireless, inexhausti-
ble, was still holding forth, endowing his thought with a
thousand sparks and as many shadows, and our common
prayer was that his voice would never stop—not before
the coming of the Messiah.

The pale dawn surprised us, filled us with a strange
happiness: together we had just traveled a long road and
shared a rare, perhaps unique, experience: the victory of
man over night. No trace of fatigue. Our faces radiated
pride. Yet my pupils, fanatically pious, had just committed a sin: for the first time in their lives, they had
forgotten to recite the evening prayer.

The Master let himself be convinced to prolong his stay
at the chateau. For a day, a week. As for me, I no longer
counted, no one invited me to put off my return; but I
stayed on anyway.

From morning to night, often until midnight and sometimes later, the Master continued to fascinate us; we were
at his mercy, he took possession of our beings, shaped
them, made them unrecognizable.

It was the month of *Av* and, out of respect for the
tradition, he spoke to us primarily of the destruction of
the Temple. I thought I knew all the legends on this subject, but in his mouth they acquired new meaning: they
made us more proud to belong to a people which had
survived its own history and still kept it so alive and so
athirst.

One day he talked to us about the secret war which

was taking place in Palestine at that time: the English were going to execute a member of the Irgun. The Master spoke of him as of a saint, elevating him to the rank of a Rebbe Akiva (who, in Roman times, had gone to his death courageously, as a free man, to glorify the name of God). If later on, I decided to join the struggle in which Jewish youth was engaging for the independence of our people, I did so because of my master.

Then came the day of departure. My pupils asked him if he intended to return. He answered: "Perhaps."

"Where are you going now? To what new adventure, what discoveries?"

"That doesn't concern you," he said, annoyed.

Then they turned toward me.

"And you, you'll come back?"

I said no.

My encounter with the Master had put an end to my career as lecturer. I became a pupil again. We left the chateau together; the students accompanied us to the station.

In the train that took us back to Paris I informed him of my decision not to leave him. He opposed this, but I stood firm.

I said: "I need you."

He retorted: "And who told you you're capable of following me? Or that you're worthy?"

"I did."

"You?" he roared. "You think you're your own master? You listen to your own voice? Where do you get such arrogance?"

"From you."

Furious, he covered me with insults, but I did not give in. I finally won out. On our arrival, as we were leaving the Gare du Nord, I followed him with a determined step.

"Where are you going?"

"With you."

"And if I say no?"

"I'll follow you anyway."

I hastened to add: "It was you who taught me the meaning of freedom."

His ugly face turned red and for a moment I thought he was going to spit in my face. But he calmed down.

"You're obstinate," he said disdainfully, "but I like Jews to be obstinate."

Then he made a gesture of discouragement. "So be it, you'll accompany me for a while." He caught himself at once: "But not now. Some other time. I'll come to see you."

"When?"

"I don't know."

"When?"

"Soon."

"In the morning? The evening?"

"How do you expect me to know that now?"

He left me near a subway station and disappeared.

In my wretched little room, in Porte Saint-Cloud, I awaited him in doubt: would he keep his promise? I dared not leave, not even to go to the bakery. Three days later, he knocked at my door. He inspected the premises, cast a look of disgust at the books, and ordered me to sit on the bed. He took the only chair in the room for himself.

"Look at me and listen without interrupting."

He came back twice a week, never the same day, never the same hour. Sometimes he came early in the morning, while the city was still sleeping; at other times, he seemed to draw the twilight in behind him. He stayed three hours, four, five, six. A day, a century, for him it was all the same: he denied time. As soon as he arrived he began to speak on whatever subject preoccupied him that day. And each time I felt the same sense of amazement.

Later I learned that during this same period he had other disciples (Emmanuel Levinas was one), and that he devoted as many hours to them as to me. Where did he find the time and energy? I never saw him eat, sleep, or read; yet he was in the best of health and seemed well-informed about every realm of human activity. On several occasions he disappeared for a week or longer; he returned unchanged.

I was his disciple for three whole years and I know no more about him today—probably less—than at our first encounter in the small synagogue, Rue Pavé, the night I went to celebrate the splendor of Shabbat.

One day he learned of the arrival in Paris of a great Hasidic Rebbe, who was on his way to the United States. The faithful from London and Zurich, from Antwerp and Frankfort, were converging on the capital, some to greet him, some to ask his counsel and blessing.

"You know him?" asked my master.

"Yes, he comes from our region, from Transylvania. Before the war I used to see him from the distance. He wasn't my rebbe; mine was the Rebbe of Wizsnitz."

"What have you got against this one?"

"Nothing, except that he didn't suffer—or rather, he didn't suffer enough—during the war."

"And you? Did you suffer enough?"

"No, not enough. But I'm not anyone's rebbe."

"How do you know?"

He was going to launch one of his poisoned darts, but he restrained himself.

"You attach too much importance to suffering."

I waited for him to continue, he did not. That day, preoccupied by the Rebbe, he spared me.

"I want to get to know him," my master said.

"That won't be easy."

The Rebbe was staying at a luxurious hotel on the Right Bank. There were crowds in the corridors. People waited on line for hours, and an audience lasted no more than five minutes. Before penetrating the salon where the holy man was holding court, one had to give the secretary in the antechamber a *pidyon*, a banknote. This was the custom: before seeing the Rebbe in person, one had to perform a good deed—giving alms was an example—to earn such an honor.

"Come with me," the Master ordered.

I feared the worst. Would the doorman let a hobo and his servant enter? That day no one stopped us at the entrance. A bellboy took one look at us and immediately said: "He's on the second floor." Three hundred people were packed into the corridor. My master cleared a passageway to the secretary: "I want to see him."

"Wait on line like everyone else."

"I'm not someone to be included with 'everyone else.' "

"Well, so you won't see him."

"Really?"

He tore a sheet of paper from my notebook, scribbled a few words.

"I order you to give this message to the Rebbe, otherwise I'll curse you."

The secretary obeyed. What is even stranger—the door opened and the Rebbe himself came out to ask my master to join him inside. They conversed several hours alone and the matters they discussed were never divulged. After having said good-bye to him, the Rebbe was content to murmur:

"I realize a human being can know so many things, but how do you manage to understand them all?"

Later, I asked my master: "What did you write in your message?"

"That's of no concern to you."

"It's just that I'd like to know how to open certain doors."

He became angry.

"That isn't anything one can learn. You'd want to imitate me? It's not by imitating anyone that you'll open anything at all. One doesn't buy keys, one makes them for himself. What makes up my strength may produce nothing but grief for you. The duty of a disciple is to follow his master, not to copy him."

Fortunately his fits of anger quickly subsided. They came over him and departed as quickly, bringing him, illuminated, back to himself.

Only once did he go away foaming with rage, slamming the door behind him. That, too, was my fault. I had violated his sanctuary; I had asked him the question that kept coming back to me, even in my dreams:

"Who are you? Whom are you hiding? Why do you make such a mystery of yourself? Do you really believe that it is man's duty to withdraw into himself rather than to open himself up to others?"

He stiffened. His breath became heavy, his face cruel. He scrutinized me in silence, looking for a way to wound me, to kill me perhaps. Panic-stricken, I tried to justify myself:

"Don't be angry with me. I'm not asking out of curiosity or indiscretion. I would simply like to know, for the future, for my children perhaps, who it was who exercised such an influence on their father."

He leaped to his feet and shook his fist at me. His wrath exploded.

"And who tells you there will be a future? And who gives you permission to dissociate me from it and speak of me in the past tense?"

No longer in control of himself, like one possessed, he began racing from one wall to another, uttering shrill cries.

He disappeared for about ten days. I was sure I would never see him again. But he reappeared and took up his instruction again as if nothing had happened, at precisely the point where we had broken off. From then on, I was very careful not to trespass forbidden ground. I thought: "If he wants to confide in me, he will not wait for my questions." Now I am inclined to think I was wrong; I should have persisted. Perhaps he was waiting for me to try him again. Sometimes I tell myself his fury was only comedy.

At the end of 1948 he left me, without saying good-bye or farewell. His last lesson was like all the others. Nothing in his conduct would have betrayed his intention to sever our ties. He was neither more cheerful nor sadder than ever. As usual, I accompanied him to the subway station and as usual he advised me to go back.

"Think over my lesson and try to destroy it."

He did not return.

A week passed; he gave no further sign of life. Another week; no one knocked at my door. I set out to look for him in all the synagogues: to no avail. In the hospitals, everywhere, no patient answered his description.

I knew it was hopeless. No use to go against his will, against his freedom. Our relationship had to be onesided.

At loose ends, unprotected, friendless, I decided to leave France. They were fighting in Israel and I was burning to go there, I was restless. It was not until later, much later, that I learned that he too had responded to the same call, at just about the same time, a bit earlier.

I did not remain long in the Holy Land, he neither. For no reason travel appealed to me; I was pursuing someone without knowing whom. Now I tell myself it was him. But our paths never crossed again. Yet he too had taken up once more the pilgrim's staff.

From time to time I meet a friend who knew him in the thirties, the forties, the fifties, in Paris or Jerusalem, in New York or Algeria. We spend the whole night evoking his image. At times it is a stranger who speaks to me of him; then we become friends.

Recently, in a plane taking me from Buenos Aires to New York, a passenger told me that a peculiar character had turned up, in the early sixties, in Montevideo. The

Master was leading the same life there as in France. His physical appearance had remained the same, so too his intellectual enterprise. The passionate mystery surrounding him and which he harbored remained intact. He was believed to be the guardian of an unfathomable secret. One day he would demonstrate his superiority over the scholars and the rabbis; the next he would perform the beadle's job and demand that he be subjected to servitude and humiliation. No one there, or anywhere else, ever knew what drove him to shake up so many souls and what powers he was defying. Everywhere, when he appeared, people grew silent, as if in the presence of someone who knew why we live and why we die.

Often I am seized by the desire to take the first plane leaving for Uruguay, to see him one last time to confront him with the image I have kept of him. Then too I need him to rouse me again, to suspend me between heaven and earth and so permit me to see what brings them together and what separates them.

But I am afraid. Would I find him identical with that person who overturned my life in that small synagogue in Paris, in the garden of the chateau in Taverny? Paris has changed, Taverny too, our pupils have changed: some have become rabbis in their turn, others have fallen on the battlefields of Galilee, the Negev, Jerusalem. I too, I have changed. Not he. Even the holocaust has left him intact.

That is what troubles me and frightens me: are the events which have turned my life upside-down without scratching his, are they perhaps futile, devoid of meaning? Have I then lived under the sign of error?

If, for him, the past is nothing, the future is nothing, then is death nothing either and the death of a million Jewish children? Perhaps God is dead, but he does not know it; and if he does know it, he acts as if it is of no concern to him at all. . . .

That is what makes me tremble each time I think of him in Montevideo, where he awaits me, where he calls to me: I am afraid to plunge once more into his legend which condemns us both, me to doubt, and him to immortality.

11.
The Last Return

Somewhere in Transylvania, in the shadow of the Carpathians, very near the most capricious frontier of Eastern Europe, there is a dusty little town called Sighet. It is a town like many others, and yet it is not like any other. Quiet, withdrawn, resigned, it seems almost petrified in its own forgetfulness; and in the shame that springs from that forgetfulness. It has denied its past; it is condemned to live outside of time; it breathes only in the memory of those who have left it.

This was my town once; it is not my town now. And yet it has scarcely changed at all since I left it twenty years ago. The low, gray houses are still there. The church and the butcher shop are still facing each other. The synagogue, deserted now, still stands at the corner of the little market square.

It is this fidelity to its own image that makes the town seem strange to me. By looking like itself, it has betrayed itself. It has lost the right to its name and to its destiny. Sighet is not Sighet any more.

For a long time I had had a burning desire to go there. For a week, an hour, a minute—just long enough for a single look. To see it one last time and then to depart, never to see it again.

Nowadays, in spite of the Iron Curtain, distances no longer matter. Anyone at all may leave from anywhere at all and arrive at Sighet, by way of Bucharest, Cluj, and Baia-Mare, by airplane, by train, by car, in less than seventy-two hours. But not I. For me the journey was longer. It was to take me back to where everything began, where the world lost its innocence and God lost his mask. It was from Sighet that I started on my journey to Sighet.

For twenty years I had done nothing but prepare for this journey. Not with joy—on the contrary, with anguish. In a dim way I felt where the danger lay: this pilgrimage would be a watershed. From that time on there would be a "before" and an "after." Or rather, there would no longer be a "before." What would be waiting for me when I arrived? The dead past or the past revived? Total desolation or a city rebuilt again and a life once more become normal? For me, in either case, there would be despair. One cannot dig up a grave with impunity. The secret of the *Maase-B'reshit*, the beginning of all things, is guarded by the Angel of Death. One approaches it only at the risk of losing his last tie to the earth, his last illusion, his faith, or his reason.

After the liberation, at Buchenwald, the Americans wanted to repatriate me. I objected. I did not like the idea of living alone in an abandoned place. They insisted: "Do you mean to say you refuse to go home?" I no longer had a home, I said. "And you're not curious to go back and see the place where you were born, where you spent your childhood?" No, I did not know what curiosity was anymore. And besides, that town they were talking about no longer existed. It had followed the Jew into deportation.

I preferred to exile myself to France. I began wandering all over the world. To Israel, to America, to the Far East. Far away, as far as possible. Unable to remain in any one place, I ran from one country to another, from one experience to another, never knowing whether it was in order to get away from Sighet, or to find it again. The town haunted me, I saw it everywhere, always the same as it had been. It invaded my dreams, it came between me and the world, between me and other people, between me and myself. By trying to free myself from it, I was becoming its prisoner.

The town fascinated me and frightened me. I wanted and did not want to see it again. Sometimes I told myself: "The war is nothing but a bad dream: soon, when I awake, the moment I return, I shall find the place just as I knew it, with its *yeshivot*, its stores, its Talmudists, its merchants, its beggars, and its madmen. And I shall feel guilty for having dreamed that they were dead."

At other times I had the opposite vision: I would be the only one to return, I would walk through the streets, aimless, without seeing a familiar face, an open look. And I would go mad with loneliness.

More than once, I was on the verge of undertaking this journey; at the last moment I would invent some pretext for putting it off. Later. Next month, next year. I did not have the courage, the strength. I sometimes found myself thinking: "Who knows, perhaps I have never left it." Or else: "Perhaps it never existed outside my own imagination." Or again: "Perhaps the whole universe is nothing but a phantasmagorical projection of Sighet; perhaps the whole universe is turning into Sighet."

Then, one day, I decided that twenty years was enough. I set out. I do not know whether I did right; no doubt I shall never know. I searched in Sighet for those who might have advised me or enlightened me, but I did not find them. They had not come back.

In 1944 Sighet was part of Hungary; today it belongs to Rumania. To get there, I took a plane from Bucharest as far as Baia-Mare. At Baia-Mare, I hired a taxi to cross the mountains. One hundred fifty kilometers: six hours, fifteen dollars. Although the driver was pleased to earn so much money so quickly—it is as much as a laborer makes in one week—he seemed sullen and taciturn. He did not like driving at night across the mountains. The roads were badly lit and in poor condition.

"Do you know Sighet?"

"Yes."

"What do you think of it?"

"Why, it's just a town, a town like any other."

"Tell me about it. What does it look like?"

"There's nothing to tell."

"Are there still Jews living there?"

"Jews? I don't know any."

He was in no mood to chat, only to curse.

For my own part, I have a great deal to tell. It sometimes seems to me that ever since I left it, I have been spending all my time telling about this town which gave me everything and then took it all away. As a boy, I was a devoted Hasid of the Wizsnitzer Rebbe, but I frequented the other Rebbes too, listened to their stories, learned their chants, ready always to catch fire wherever the spark might be found. Later, I became the disciple of a kabbalist. Every night at midnight, he would arise to put a handful of ashes on his brow; in a low voice, seated on the ground, he would lament the destruction of the Temple of Jerusalem, as well as the suffering of the *Shekhina*, which was in exile like us, with us. I was young then and could not imagine that the Temple would soon be destroyed six million times, that the suffering of God could never—never—be compared to that of the Jewish children who were already being sent to the pyre while the world remained silent, as silent as he who is judged to be its creator.

"We're coming near," said the driver. Where were we? At the foot of the mountain, thank God. The danger was past, we were in the valley. Sighet: 40 kilometers. Sighet: 30 kilometers. A multitude of huts formed a hedge along the road. Villages sprang up before our headlights and were immediately swallowed again by the night. Far away, there were a few blinking lights. Sighet: 20 kilometers. The car, an old Volga, picked up speed. Sighet: 15 kilometers. "We're coming near," the driver repeated in a heavy voice. His words sounded like a threat. He was taking me to a rendezvous. With whom? With death? With myself? Sighet: 10 kilometers. Sighet: twenty years.

I entered the town as one enters a dream: gliding forward noiselessly, without resistance, accepting in advance the best and the worst. Holding my breath, I exploded in time, which was torn apart into a thousand fragments, a thousand faces. The dead on one side, I on the other. Spring, 1944—autumn, 1964. I had left by train, I was coming back by car. The only difference was that it had been warm on that day with the fragrant promise of summer; now it was cold, it was almost winter, it was night. Yet the beginning and the end came strangely together, tracing a circle of fire which became smaller and smaller: I was caught inside, too late to escape.

"Here we are," said the driver. His hand open, he asked for his money; he was in a hurry, he had to return to Baia-Mare. I asked him: "Are you sure this is Sighet? The former capital of Maramures?" He said yes, but I did not trust him. The town looked like Sighet, but that did not prove anything. There was the main street, the movie theater, the hotel, the girls' high school. Across from me was the street called the Jews' Street. On the right, the stores; further on, on the left, the courthouse. Nothing had changed? Nothing. Then why did I feel like the victim of a ludicrous misunderstanding? Someone had deceived me: the driver, for his own amusement, had deposited me in a strange town. And if not he, then it was another driver, more powerful and more cruel, more cunning too, who was laughing at my expense. "Are you really sure? You're not fooling me?" He grinned and reassured me, but I did not believe him, I did not believe myself. His voice was lying, my eyes were lying. This town was lying. It was called Sighet—well, what of it? That meant nothing: a false name, a false identity. Sighet, the real Sighet, was elsewhere, somewhere in Upper Silesia, near a peculiar little railroad station called Birkenau, near a great fire lighting up the sky; the real Sighet formed part of an immense city of ashes.

It was late, the townspeople were all asleep. Suitcase in hand, I stood on the sidewalk, with my back to the hotel, unable to move a step. Then I shook myself: start remembering. You came back here to remember—well, then, look and listen. The main square, do you remember it? When the Jews were taken to the railroad station, to the transports, the line wound all around that square. When the policemen set up the itinerary, they followed the instructions of a certain Adolf Eichmann, who had come in person to supervise the operation. Our neighbors had already descended like hungry vultures on the abandoned dwellings: there was loot free for the taking, enough for everybody, for all tastes. The police were busy elsewhere. The looters had an easy job. Observing a tacit agreement, the rich robbed the rich, while the poor took things only from the poor. After all, the natural order must prevail.

Now, there I was at the very center of the main square, standing alone like a conqueror. They had not known that I would come back, and I had come back. A supreme victory—a unique victory. Why, then, was I unable to feel any pride? It was too late. Too late for conquest, and too late for pride.

My eyes searched the house fronts with their indistinct outlines, the sightless windows, the roofs on which tall chimneys rose like specters. I was looking for a reference point, a familiar feature; there was nothing. The town hid from my glance as it hid from the light; it drew away, it shrank back. The meeting would not take place: one of the parties had failed to appear at the rendezvous.

I was no longer sure of anything. I began to doubt myself again. What had I in common with the unsophisticated little boy, in love with religion and with the Absolute, who had been driven away from this very spot more than twenty years earlier?

Silence. There had been silence on the day of our departure too. The military police, mad with rage, had run bellowing in all directions and struck at men, women, children, not so much to hurt them as to make them groan. But the crowd had been mute. Not one cry, not one complaint. An old man, wounded in the head, had risen to his feet again and bitten his lip. A woman, her face full of blood, had walked on without slowing her pace. The town had never before known such a silence. Not a sigh, not a sound. Silence: the perfect setting for the last scene of the last act. The Jews were retiring from the scene. Forever.

I remembered that walking with the crowd toward the

railroad station, where the sealed trains were already waiting for us, it had come into my mind that the silence would triumph, that it was stronger than we, stronger than they; it was beyond language, beyond lies, beyond time; it drew its strength from the very struggle which pitted life against its negation, brutality against silent prayer. Or was I just imagining that I had thought this? I did not know: I did not even know whether that young boy turning his back on his childhood, his home, his chance for happiness, had really been myself. Somewhere along the way, between the synagogue and the railroad station, between the station and the unknown, he had been killed. It might even be that I had killed him myself.

It was almost midnight now: I had to hurry. I had dawdled too long, I had not accomplished anything yet. There was not another minute to lose. Do something quickly. But just what? Something that will measure up to the return, if not to the departure. Awake the dead, perhaps. Or else set fire to the town, send it to join those who were gone, and let the army of shadows be victorious. Or, again, simply start singing or laughing. Just like that, in the street, in the cold. Until morning comes.

I crossed over to the hotel. A shabby, dilapidated entrance, a stairway with no railing, a dim light. Could this be the famous Hotel Corona? With my Jewish child's eyes I had seen it—from the outside, from afar—as a palace reserved for princes from distant lands: high officials on inspection trips, General Staff officers on special missions, fabulously rich American women visiting their families. The Hotel Corona had meant luxury, fulfilled desire, glory, light-heartedness, liberty, vice.

Today the hotel is all "people," "working class," "peace," "socialism." Like everything else, it had lied to the child I had been; it was without pomp, without comfort.

In his glass-enclosed cage on the second floor, muffled in a thick blanket, the night clerk saw me approaching. His face was ageless and expressionless, his eyes absent and indifferent. I asked for a room. Had I a reservation? No. That was a pity: no reservation, no room. Why not? Was the hotel full, perhaps? Not at all, it was empty. I did not understand, and he explained that it was the rule. I gave him a tip, which took care of the rule. Very well, now I had to fill out the police form, that was the law. Sighet was a frontier town, no one could stay there for four hours without advising the Militia. The clerk took out a large register and began writing. Family name, given name, family status, occupation, place of residence. "New York," I said. He dropped his pen and stared at me. "You came from New York? To Sighet?" I answered, "Yes, from New York to Sighet." His surprise grew when he learned that I had been born in Sighet. Bewildered, he looked me over curiously. What did I want here at Sighet, so late at night, in this mournful hotel? Finally, he gave me a room: if I did not like it, I could choose another. I asked for a towel, and again he stared at me. Quite definitely, he did not like my behavior, and he would not forget to mention this detail in his report to the Militia; one never knew, it might be significant. I told him, "All right, don't bother, I'll do without the towel. Anyhow, I'm going right out again." Convinced that I was making fun of him, he opened his mouth to ask me something, but I did not give him the chance. I was already on my way down the stairs, seeking the outside air, the deserted and silent main square. Once outside, I took a deep breath: and now where?

To my house, of course—home at last. Light the candles, set the table for the feast of reunion. The wandering son has returned. Will you find the way in the dark? Nothing simpler, my legs will take me there. My legs have a better memory than my eyes anyway; they never had to look upon those clouds of smoke, those clouds in which an entire people, bound together, rose up.

I stepped forward slowly, cautiously. The firehouse, where was the firehouse? It should be at the corner of the main street. Swallowed up. And the booth on the corner, at the entrance to the Jews' Street? Old Semel used to sell his fruit there, summer and winter; now there was no booth, no fruit, no Semel. Further on, the church. That was still there, thank God. And the house, my house? I tried to calm myself, but I was afraid—of seeing it again, of not seeing it again. Don't run, don't run, neither forward nor back: what is the point of running anymore? But my legs refused to obey. They ran, they flew. And I flew—above the roofs, above the memories. Houses, trees, chimneys, clouds, windows, all flew with me toward a vanished town, toward a stolen house. As my legs were seized with flight, my throat was seized with an irresistible desire to shout, to tear the night apart, to make the earth tremble once and for all, to make the heavens fall. But I no longer had any control over my body. I shouted, but no sound came out. The town went on sleeping, with no fear of the silence.

I ran, as a convict runs toward freedom, as a madman runs toward his madness; I ran even while I knew that no one and nothing was waiting for me over there, at the end of the run, over there in the building at the intersection of the two streets, facing the police station. If my house had survived the flames of madness, if it was still standing, a curse be upon it: strangers were living in it.

Here it was.

All at once, I had only one desire, to stretch out on the sidewalk, to rest, to catch my breath, no longer to run, no longer to think, no longer to play the phantom among men, no longer to play the man among men. The play was over. Curtain. The player was tired; the spectator was exhausted; go home to bed, we are closing, save your strength, tomorrow will be another day. But I remained on my feet, stretched tight like a bow with arrows pointed at myself. I looked and listened as I had never looked and listened in my life. The imperceptible noises, the wavering shadows, the secret vibrations—I captured them, I interrogated them, I imprisoned them, I made them mine.

The street, the house: there they were, mine again. More than before, better than ever. Total, irrevocable possession: more than when I had lived there. My walls, my neighbors, my garden, my trees, my witnesses, my murderers, my playmates, my classmates. For a long moment I wandered around the building with its drawn curtains. I asked myself whether I should not simply knock on the window and wake up the residents: "Let me in, I'll go away tomorrow." I knew that I would not do it, and I felt humiliated and defeated.

Like a blind man, I let my fingers wander over the fence that surrounded the garden, over the walls of the house, over the windows; I was waiting for them to return to me the things that had strayed, the images that had dissolved. I felt vulnerable and invincible at the same time: I could do everything, I could do nothing. I could evoke the past, I could not bring it to life again. Nothing had changed. The house was the same, the street was the same, the world was the same, God was the same. Only the Jews had disappeared.

I told myself that I should open the gate, go across the yard, walk up to the porch, go into the kitchen. Who could tell? Perhaps someone was waiting for me near the stove, someone who would not ask me any questions but would invite me to sit down at the table, offer me a glass of milk and a piece of bread, and say: "You are exhausted, the bed is ready, go and rest, you have traveled a long way."

But I knew that the one who was sleeping in my bed would not forgive me for having come back. Perhaps he was not even asleep; perhaps he had been watching for my return for twenty years. Better to go away, leave the town, the country. What more had I to see here?

Strange: I had come from very far away to take one more look at the house, the yard, the well near the cellar, the garden—and I could not manage to step through the gate. From far away the yard had never seemed so inaccessible to me. Stiffening, holding my breath, I forced my hand onto the iron door-handle, caressing it ever so gently before turning it. My shoulder pushed the gate, which gave a familiar little squeak as it opened up just wide enough for me to slip inside. Then, closing the gate again, I leaned on it with my full weight, my heart beating violently, my head bursting with delirium. The yard—our yard. Nothing had been moved out of place. The empty barrel at the entrance to the cellar, the empty bucket hanging above the well, the tree with its withered arms turned toward the garden: I could see them all through seven layers of darkness. The only thing that remained for me to do was to go into the kitchen, from there to the living room, and then into the bedroom.

But I did not do it. It was the sharp, nervous bark of a dog that stopped me. I had expected everything but that. There had never been any dog in the house. We Jewish children had been taught to fear dogs; they were friends of the enemy, all demons, all anti-Semitic. Invaded by the absurd old terror, I bolted through the gate and onto the sidewalk: driven out a second time. By a dog, the true victor in this war. I took to flight, as I had long ago. I ran to the main street, to the main square; for lack of any other refuge, I collapsed on a bench and dropped my head onto my hands, blinded by pain, by rage, by shame —especially by shame. As I sat there, a new day began to dawn on the summit of the mountain.

I had lived through my return to Sighet long before it actually took place. I had described it in my novel *The Town Beyond the Wall*. Retrospectively, the novel became a report. Except for the events of the night, nothing was missing. In the morning I picked up the thread of the book: I used it as a guide. Seen in daylight the town appeared to me exactly as I had dreamed it: bare, without any vigor, without any mystery.

As in the novel, it was an autumn morning. The weather was fine. A yellow sun was advancing across the grayish-blue sky. Yellow, too, was the foliage; yellow the walls of the buildings; yellow the dead leaves; yellow, sad, discouraged were the men and women going to work, to market, to church, the children going to school.

I looked into the eyes of the people I met—would I recognize anyone? A friend? An enemy? A neighbor? No, I had never seen any of them before. I did not know them, they did not know me. Some of them looked at me without seeing me, fleetingly; others saw me without looking at me, their thoughts elsewhere. No one approached me, no one turned his head. Not one gesture of astonishment or complicity. Nothing. They showed neither pleasure nor disappointment: my return was of no consequence to them. I had survived, that was my affair, not theirs. If I had spoken to them, they would have continued on their way; if I had started yelling "Disgrace!" or "Fraud!" they would not even have shrugged their shoulders. As if I did not exist. Or rather, as if I had never existed.

I scrutinized the passersby with fascination. Former classmates? Former friends of my friends? Former customers of my father? To which of them had we entrusted our Sabbath candelabra, our winter clothes, our valuable papers? An old housewife was returning from market: wasn't that Mrs. Stark, who had agreed to keep our sewing machine in her house? An energetic-looking official was coming out of the courthouse: wasn't that the generous lawyer to whom we had "sold" some of our pieces of property? A man about my age was talking to his son, showing him some object in the window of the old pastry

shop that had belonged to the Stein family: wasn't that
Pishta the Swaggerer, the very same one who used to go
about dressed up as a demon on Christmas week, a whip
in his hand, punishing any Jew he found for having killed
his God? Ready to catch the slightest sign, the slightest
blink of an eye, I mingled with the people in the street, in
the stores, in the market. I brushed against them, I
bumped into them: no one paid any attention.

They should have inspired anger and bitterness in me,
moved me to contempt. But I felt nothing of the sort. I
was surprised to find myself sharing their indifference.
Passing my house again, I saw the man who was living in
it come out, a young engineer of Hungarian origin, with a
lively glance, full of vigor: I said nothing to him. He
would have replied: "I'm sorry." No, not even that. He
would have said nothing. He would not have remembered
me. No more than the others would. More than anywhere
else, it was at Sighet that I understood that the Jews had
lost the war.

And yet I was not angry with the people of Sighet.
Neither for having driven out their neighbors of yester-
day nor for having denied them. If I was angry at all, it
was rather for having forgotten them.

So quickly, so completely.

Long ago, in this typical *shtetl*, Israel had been king.
Although a minority in a town of twenty-five thousand,
Sighet's ten thousand Jews had set the tone in everything.
As everywhere else in Central Europe, the Jews served
as a measure, a barometer. The rich Jews were richer
than the others, the poor Jews were poorer. In good and
in bad, they lived in a constant state of excess.

In the thirties, my father had turned down an American visa, saying: "Why look for America in America,
when it is right here?"

During the first years of the war certain rumors

reached us concerning what was happening in Poland; among the Jews of Sighet these rumors roused very little anxiety—and even that was quickly forgotten. The rabbis said: "Nothing will happen to us, for God needs us." The merchants said: "The country needs us." The doctors said: "The town needs us." They all considered themselves indispensable and irreplaceable.

In 1943 it was possible to obtain "certificates" for Palestine: nobody wanted any. No, that is not true: one single Jew decided to go there. The others smiled: "Why leave? We are all right here, the people are friendly, they cannot do without us and they know it."

In Poland, in the Ukraine, in Germany, earth and sky had been burning for a long time, there were almost no Jews left there, but to us the world looked stable. The danger had not forced its way into our consciousness or disturbed our sleep. In the *yeshivot,* the young boys studied the Talmud; in the *heder* the children were learning the *aleph-bet;* in the stores people were buying, selling, competing for customers; on the Jews' Street, during the idle hours, people were discussing politics, finance, marriage, strategy, Hasidism, and if anyone had dared to suggest that the day was coming when the town would get rid of the Jews as though they were a pack of lepers, they would have laughed in his face.

Everyone had faith in the future. They were sure that life would go on that way eternally. A teacher explained to his pupils: "Do you know what the eternity of God is? It is we. By dancing on fire, by facing suffering and death, man creates the eternity of his creator—he offers it to him and justifies it."

Then came the German occupation. It happened at the beginning of 1944, a few days before Passover. Faces grew dark. Suddenly the Christian population dropped its mask—and declared its thirst for Jewish blood. But still the Jews assured one another: "It will pass, we must be patient and not despair."

The Festival of Freedom was celebrated while we waited for an event that nobody was able or willing to foresee.

Eternity ended one month later.

But not for Sighet. The town has twenty-five thousand inhabitants again. They lead a normal existence. With no Jewish doctors, no Jewish merchants, no Jewish shoemakers. People get along without them, they are not missed. The gap was quickly filled. All the apartments are occupied, the schools are full, the stores have been taken over by the state. The Jewish community numbers less than fifty families, and most of them come from other places.

There is even talk of progress. Several large buildings have gone up recently. An elementary school, a cooperative, a textile plant—the pride of the town. One more proof that people do not need Jews at all in order to march with the times, to conquer the future.

If I had been a simple tourist, I would have had to admire the achievements of the new regime. But I was not. More than the night before, I felt myself a stranger, if not an intruder, in this sinister town which was stripped of all vigor, of any life of its own. I searched for the people out of my past, I searched for my past, and I did not find them. Why was everything so calm in front of the Talmud-Torah Synagogue and the Machzikei-Torah Synagogue and the Wizsnitzer *shtibel?* I looked for Kalman the Kabbalist, Moshe the Madman, Shmukler the Prince, Leizer the Fat: vanished without a trace as though carried off by one of the "anti-personnel" neutron bombs that destroy people and spare the stones they call their property.

Incredulously, I visited all the places which had once filled my landscape: unchanged, anonymous. I stopped in front of my grandmother's house; I stopped in front of the store once owned by my uncle, a learned Talmudist and a wretched merchant; I stopped in front of my teacher's house. A thousand adventures, all with the same end.

I walked from one synagogue to another; the biggest and oldest of them no longer existed: it had been destroyed by the retreating Germans, and a commemorative stone had been erected above its ruins. The others were empty, abandoned, cluttered with sacred books piled up helter-skelter and covered with dust. One single synagogue, too spacious for the fifty Jews who assemble there on Rosh Hashana, remained open.

The Jews' Street, once so lively and noisy, is now deserted. Its name has been changed. It is called the Street of the Deported. Who deported whom? A question devoid of interest or importance. No one asks it. The past is buried. People must live. And above all, they must forget. I met my old elementary-school teacher: my name meant nothing to him. I spoke to a neighbor who used to come to us every day of the week: she did not remember me. Some day some worthy citizen will glance at the name of the business street and say quite innocently: "The Street of Deported? I seem to recall that they were Jews." He will not be sure. Even today he is not sure. The Jews deported from Sighet did not belong to Sighet. They belonged to some other place, some other planet. They were strangers. If the Jews were to come back, they would be driven away again.

Had it not ever been thus? No doubt it had, but I had been too young at the time to understand it. The population had always thought that Jews did not become strangers, they were born that way. Only, these peaceful inhabitants go further than that. Today, for them, I am not even a stranger robbed of his childhood, not even a phantom in search of memories. Have they forgotten everything? No. Rather, they give the impression of having nothing to forget. There never were any Jews in Sighet, the former capital of the celebrated region of Maramures.

Thus, the Jews have been driven not only out of the town but out of time as well.

The only place where I felt at home, on familiar ground, was the Jewish cemetery. And yet I had never set foot in it before. Children had been forbidden to enter. Why? Because. When you grow up, you'll understand. I would imagine the dead conversing with God, or I would be among them, brushing against the walls, keeping my ears open; I wanted to listen, but there had always been someone to send me back to school or back home. Now I was free to enter. There was no longer anyone to tell me what was permitted and what was not. I had grown up.

This was the only place in Sighet that reminded me of Sighet, the only thing that remained of Sighet. Outside, I was on foreign soil; here I was in the bosom of a great and powerful family ready to welcome me, to protect me.

Perhaps it was simply because the dead who were here had been luckier than the others. They had not been deported. Remaining where they were, they had not had to undergo any humiliation. They had been let alone, left in peace. Perhaps that was why I had come to them: not so much to bid them farewell as to entrust them with the town, with the town's Jewish past.

I wandered from one grave to another. I had bought some candles. I lit them, placing one wherever I found a familiar name. The wind blew them out. I struggled against it, in vain.

In the old days people had come here from far and near, especially between Rosh Hashana and Yom Kippur, to lie down on the graves of the *Tzadikim* and implore them to intercede with the heavenly power to stop pursuing the people who had been too much chosen for too much suffering. Useless prayers, useless tears. The intercession had done no good. God had closed his ears and let it all happen.

Finally, I stopped in front of a monument to the memory of a generation that had died elsewhere. A slanting block of stone, with a few words engraved on it. A tomb with no corpses. A gravestone with no graves instead of innumerable graves. I held a match to the last candle. To my great surprise, the wick caught at the first attempt and flamed upward. Was it a miracle? Would the flame rise to the seventh heaven and still higher to the tenth sphere, and still higher, to the celestial throne, and still higher than that?

Suddenly I was aware of a presence—an old Jew was standing at my side. Without greeting me, without saying a word, he took a *siddur* from his pocket and began to recite the funeral chant: *El mole rachamim shokhen bimromim.* Where had this apparition come from? How had he found out I was there? I do not know. Perhaps he came to the cemetery day after day for the sole purpose of praying that all the Jews of Sighet, swallowed up by the night, might at last rest in peace. As he prayed I closed my eyes and shame came over me again.

The last candle burned for a long time. Sometimes I tell myself that it is still burning.

I met a second Jew in front of the Sephardic synagogue. The very sight of this extraordinary person, this bearded man dressed like a Hasid, took me back twenty years. I accosted him in Yiddish. Surprised, he shook my hand and looked at me lingeringly. *Sholem aleichem, aleichem sholem:* Peace be with you, my companion. A bond was established at once. Simple answers to harmless questions. No, he was not from Sighet. No, he had never known my father. What was he doing in this de-Judaized town? He was attending to the living. A rabbi? No. A *shamash*—a sexton? No. Was he teaching children the sacred language? No, not that either. Besides, there were no longer any children who would be willing to learn it.

"I am the *shochet*," he said—the ritual slaughterer. Incredible but true; in Sighet and the surrounding villages there were still Jews who ate kosher food. Not many. Ten here, ten there. At Borshe, a mountain town, there were not more than five. Three at Stremtere, another three at Dragmerest. It was for their sake that he had decided to stay, after sending his wife and children abroad; he would go to join them only when nobody here needed his services. For the moment he did not consider himself free. Going from village to village, from house to house, he did his work without complaint—on the contrary, he said he was happy, for he was more useful here than he could be anywhere else.

I gazed at him in silence. I felt like giving him everything I possessed, but he had no need of anything. In the face of such generosity, a man feels poor; in the face of such humility, he feels humble. "I could not make up my mind to go," he told me, smiling. "After all, I could not abandon an entire Jewish community that way, without a *shochet*." He did not realize how much cruelty was contained in his words. Fifty families, a community. And to think that long ago this community had been a center of learning, a wellspring of life and wealth.

If the legend of the Thirty-six Just Men is true, this slaughterer is one of them.

Twenty-four hours after arriving in the town, I hastened to leave. One dawn, one dusk: that was enough. Already, remorse was coming over me: I had been wrong to come. Of the four wise men who, the Talmud tells us, made their way into the fields of knowledge, only one emerged unscathed; and even he did not dare go in again.

The car was waiting for me, the driver was impatient. "Are we leaving?" Yes, we were leaving. Was it fatigue that I found it so hard to lift my little suitcase, put it on the front seat, and then dump myself into the back? The slightest movement required a painful effort. A part of me wanted to remain. From here on it would be a one-way trip; every step would take me farther away from this place. "Are we leaving?" Yes, we were leaving. He let in the clutch, and the car started off. "Don't go so fast," I said in a low voice. Not so fast. I had seen everything, I wanted to see more. The little girl holding on to her mother's arm. The couple stopping in front of a store window. The policeman on duty in front of the courthouse. The passersby who had not seen me arrive and now did not see me leaving.

Here was the main street, the main square, the movie theater, the pastry shop, the girls' high school. A last glance toward my own street: the belfry of the church, the new school building, and further on, at the intersection of two streets, my house.

Sighet had long sunk below the horizon, and I still kept my head turned toward it, as though it were possible for me to carry it away in my gaze. And then I understood that I could not do so, and that in my heart I did not wish to do so. I had brought no part of it away with me, nothing but the feeling of emptiness. My journey to the source of all events had been merely a journey to nothingness.

For it had never existed—this town that had once been mine.

12.

Appointment with Hate

Seventeen years after I had left Germany—left it, as we say, forever—I went back.

I returned, in 1962, not to exorcise a few aging, probably dated demons, but to make a kind of pilgrimage to the source. The criminal is not alone when he returns to the scene of the crime; he is joined there by his victim, and both are driven by the same curiosity: to relive that moment which stamped past and future for each. So I undertook to retrace my steps, to seek a double confrontation: between them and myself, between the self I had left at Buchenwald and the other self that thought it was healed.

I came away from the confrontation with my head bowed in humiliation. I had been sure of finding my hate for Germany intact; seventeen years before I had thought it eternal. But even eternity changes its face.

After the war, I had deliberately avoided all contact with Germans. Their presence sickened me physically. The blood rushed to my head whenever I received a letter from a cousin in Frankfort. I could hardly bear it. Where Germany was concerned, logical arguments no longer had any force.

Hence it was with apprehension that I prepared for the journey to the place where my hate was waiting for me. I did not know it would break the appointment. Baudelaire calls hate a drunkard in the gloom of a tavern who can never fall asleep under the table. But there are drunkards who die in their sleep.

Yet for me the task should not have been difficult. What could be easier than to detest this people? They had started and lost the most ignominious war in history, and afterward had managed to surpass their conquerors in wealth and happiness. Above all, in complacency.

In the Paris–Stuttgart plane, a man sat beside me who was a student of philosophy at Heidelberg. He asked me what I thought his country was like. I replied: I imagine it abject and kneeling, filled with ruins and cemeteries, sobbing with fear and remorse; I imagine it famished and tormented, its inhabitants crawling on the ground, begging for pardon and oblivion. He burst out laughing. I can promise you a surprise, he said.

He was right to laugh. Of course, I was not thinking of his country's material condition, for I knew it was at the peak of its productivity. The cold war requires a "German shield," military strength matched by economic power. German industry once again plays a preponderant role in world markets, the Krupp factories work at top speed, there is no unemployment. Berlin organizes film festivals to rival those at Cannes and Venice; Volkswagens and

Mercedes streak the dusty roads of Asia, not to mention the super-highways of America. Living conditions have never been better, houses hold every comfort and convenience, the worker is better off than in France or Italy, and is, perhaps, happier too. Frankfort and Baden-Baden swarm with foreign tourists, and in Paris and Rome one tourist out of two speaks German. A journalist in Munich told me: Winning the war is good, losing it is better.

It was not all this that I found irritating, not the country's prosperity, but the people's complacency—a self-satisfaction unhaunted by the past. It is just we who think about the past. The Germans are not doing much thinking about the future either. People in Norway or Holland, for instance, seem more concerned with the fate of Berlin than do the West Germans. The Germans do not seem anxious about their split into two enemy camps and the possible danger this holds for the world. They look straight into your eyes when you talk to them, as if they have nothing to fear or hide—are accountable to no one. Ready to admit they are no longer our superiors, they insist on being our equals. The German does not permit himself to be judged, he is as good a man as any.

We—the victims—had not imagined, during the war, this is the way things would be after Germany's defeat. We were convinced a great deal of water would have to flow under the bridges of the Rhine before a member of the nation of executioners would dare look with unwavering glance into the eyes of a free man.

The Germans themselves were convinced of this. They were certain that the curse would pursue them, that they would never be allowed to forget. Fear kept them awake at night: thirst for vengeance on the part of survivors, they thought, would surely be insatiable. In the years immediately after the war, if you stopped a man in Munich or Kassel he would begin trembling and stammering: "I didn't do anything, see anything, know anything. I was at the front, in the hospital, at my office; I knew nothing of what was happening. I saw a column of smoke in the distance, but—I didn't know, no one told me."

Then came the Nuremberg Trials, and the execution of the major war criminals. The Germans could scarcely believe what they heard and saw: "Then they don't blame us? . . . They're leaving us alone, they're not going to make us pay?" When they came face to face with Jews, they could not help being suspicious. "What do they want from us, what are they up to? They can't forgive us so quickly, what's on their minds?" But finally the Germans understood they had nothing to fear, and so their fear turned into contempt. "Look at those Jews: they're not even capable of revenge!"—and a new phase began, the phase of self-justification. "If we are not judged, it is because we have done nothing, we are innocent. Hitler? The world could and should have stopped him in time; it did not, and it must share our guilt. The camps? Their existence was known in Washington, in London, in the Vatican: no voice was raised in protest against Auschwitz. The German people were not the only silent ones: great leaders accustomed to speaking in the name of conscience and of civilization were also silent. Why blame only us?"

Nevertheless, the Germans did admit a certain guilt toward the Jews. The Bonn government signed the reparations agreement with Israel and the Claims Conference in acknowledgment of that guilt—and that was that. What more did anyone want?

Why then should the Germans be embarrassed any longer before a foreign visitor, or play the innocent to impress anyone? They are as they are, and if you do not like them, too bad. They will neither change nor lie to please a foreigner. It is as if the Germans were saying to Israel: It is over, we no longer owe you anything. Israel has ceased being a moral problem for Germany—the issue is now political. The converse, unfortunately, is also true.

The Germany that swarmed with impersonators and cowardly liars during the years immediately following the capitulation of the Wehrmacht, it is that Germany that no longer exists. You no longer hear anyone cursing Hitler in the hope of exonerating himself. No one, these days, feels he has to exclaim: "It wasn't me, it was those others!" One young intellectual told me: "Hitler wasn't a bad man; he was wrong to surround himself with scum." Another repeated what Heinrich Gruber, the famous bishop of Berlin and the only German witness at the Eichmann trial, had said to a visitor from America: "Hitler was only the scourge of God to chastise his people." In which case are we permitted to judge the divine instrument?

The Germans no longer feel any shame, and they deny outsiders the right to intervene. They no longer feel they are standing at the bar of history.

I for one had no desire to argue with them. I could not imagine a dialogue was possible. Anything between us would not be words: language was already too much of a link.

But finally, if I was compelled to cut short my visit and take the plane back to Paris after forty-eight hours, it was precisely because I fell into the trap: I answered questions, I shook hands. I even smiled back. And then I could bear no more of this civilized behavior: having lost my taste for hating others, I began to hate myself.

The very first contact was indeed just as I had imagined. I shuddered as I set foot on German soil and caught sight of the police uniforms. When the customs officer questioned me in German I chose to answer in English, in brief, hostile phrases. "Nothing to declare?" he asked.

"Nothing."

"Nothing?"

"I said: nothing."

"Danke sehr, mein Herr." I shrugged and walked away
from him without another word. German politesse was
one thing I was not interested in. The customs man
stared after me—he was no longer used to this sort of
hostility.

(In New York, I had run into a different kind of official.
When I went to arrange for my trip, the head of the visa
section of the German consulate behaved with particular
arrogance. It was clear he suspected every Jew who asked
for a visa of scheming to emigrate to Germany. His interrogation was humiliating. When I objected, he furiously
reproached me for being oversensitive: he did not understand how a Jew could be oversensitive to a German who
is only trying to hurt his feelings.)

I strolled through the streets of Stuttgart, waiting for
the train to Baden-Baden. Now and then my eyes rested
on a face: "This one too?" I stared insistently at a middle-
aged man; I wanted to perceive the invisible: what had
he done during the war? Had our paths ever crossed in
the world of concentration camps? I was in enemy territory, surrounded by suspect faces: on guard, as if threatened by unknown but familiar danger.

I had been walking in silence, alone, for an hour. A
young woman came up and asked me the way to the
station. I told her I did not know, that I was a stranger.
She smiled. I almost smiled back, when my lips suddenly
froze: I became aware that I had been speaking German.

Later I allowed myself to relax. The definition of man
as a social animal—a polite animal—is true. I had mis-
takenly supposed that all definitions would have to be
revised for Germany.

In Baden-Baden I took part in the taping of a radio
program. Listening afterward I found what I heard incredible: there was no hate in my voice, not even bitterness, perhaps just a shade of the anger I was, uncon-
sciously, trying to conceal. Instead of shrieking out a

curse, I had merely murmured. It is difficult to live among men because it is difficult to keep still, Nietzsche said. But I should have kept still.

Next day I spoke in Munich. The Bechtle Verlag, my German publisher, had arranged an evening of readings. I read from the original French text of my first book, *Night*, a memoir of Auschwitz and Buchenwald, and the young novelist Peter Jokostra read the German translation. The audience listened in silence, then sat motionless for a while. I reassured myself: after all, there is a certain logic in my being here and relating to these Germans a few chapters of "our" history—our common history. But I could not shake off the uneasiness that weighed upon me. The Israeli humorist Ephraim Kishon has remarked: Logic, too, went up in smoke at Auschwitz.

I talked about literature and philosophy far into the night with a group of writers, young men between twenty and thirty. The subject of the camps came up seldom, always indirectly, elliptically. One man said to me: "It doesn't interest me; only abstract ideas are worth bothering about." Another remarked, apologetically: "Such themes are too sad. I like literature with more gaiety, more *joie de vivre*." A third said: "I heard you read tonight, but I must confess that concentration-camp literature leaves me cold, I just don't understand it."

Of course there are some German writers tormented by a guilt they shared by the mere fact of having lived under the Nazi regime—Heinrich Boll and Paul Shaluck, for example. Others live with a memory inherited from their fathers: like Günter Grass. The burden of guilt weighs sometimes heavy, sometimes more lightly. In the writings of Jokostra, Martin Walser, Alfred Andersch, or Ulrich Becher, there is, if not revolt, at least a search for justice, an authentic protest. Their heroes sit uncomfortably in their skins, feeling their corruption. Yet these writers, for

the most part, do not truly represent the younger generation. The members of that group have adopted a quasi-
Brechtian attitude, seeing and judging the past from a
distance, not in order to comprehend it better but to
prove that they have nothing in common with it. Novelists like Hans Christian Kirsch or Uwe Johnson turn their
backs on the Nazi period as something alien to them. In
the schools, there is rarely a mention of what the Jewish
Question was under Hitler. Dachau for the young students is the name of a peaceful village: the word has no
other ring. Auschwitz is . . . ancient history. Yet these
students have to be told something, and they are told that
it is true the Nazis mistreated the Jews: but the teachers
do not go into indelicate detail. Even if they did, the
students would not be interested—it is all dead and gone
and they can pass their tests and make their way in life
without such knowledge.

I had imagined an angry German youth. I had seen
reports of students making pilgrimages to Bergen-Belsen
and shedding bitter tears at performances of *The Diary of
Anne Frank*. If any youth had the right, even the urgent
duty, to fling its rage into the face of its parents, it was
surely the youth of Germany. Should not a young German be permitted to accuse his father? So I had imagined. But nothing I saw or heard in Germany, and virtually nothing I read bears witness to an angry youth: there
is more anger in the youth of France or England or the
United States. One exception is Günter Grass. He describes, in his *The Tin Drum*, a dwarf who refuses to
grow, or talk, or escape his condition: in this way he
judges his contemporaries, who may criticize the present
regime but think it political whimsey to bother about what
went before.

To be sure, the intellectual elite tries here and there to
sound the alarm. Lectures are held, and books dealing
with Jewish subjects are published. Martin Buber has for
some time now been glorified, *Exodus* appeared on the

best-seller lists, and translations have been prepared of the works of Sholem Aleichem and Mendele Mocher Sforim. To all this the general population continues to remain indifferent. It is not good breeding, in today's Germany, to discuss Buchenwald. If Schwarz-Bart's *The Last of the Just* achieved only limited sales in Germany as compared with its reception in other countries, it was because it contained an indictment of those who made Ernie Levy their victim. The works of Paul Rassinier sell better and are more praised. In his three so-called historical sketches, this author claims to "prove" that the Nazi liquidation of the European Jews was only a myth invented by the Zionists and their friends. According to him, the Nazis did not kill off six million Jews—a few hundred thousand at the most. Gas chambers?—pure fantasy. The Germans, young and old, like to hear a "Herr Professor"—Rassinier is a professor and French—tell them such things. It reassures them. If, at a certain period, the Germans were in bad odor the world over, it was not their fault: blame the Jews.

Suddenly, I no longer knew why I had come. To tell them about the camps? Convince them that such things had really existed? To describe the Nazi era which was, in Malraux's phrase, a "time of scorn"? I did nothing of the kind.

Aside from that one reading of a few pages of *Night*, I treated Auschwitz as taboo. I found absurd the notion that a Jewish writer should come and tell the Germans about their crimes. *Reveal*, perhaps, but tell? What was there that had not already been told? Each time my interlocutors out of politeness tried to broach the subject, I changed it. But it was only later that I understood why: I was no longer capable of hating.

A few months before, at a party in New York, a young woman had come up to me and said: "Deep down, I'm afraid of you. I know you hate me." I was stunned: "Why should I hate you?" She was of German origin, she confessed. I blushed: "Of course I couldn't hate you, you're too lovely." She was in fact known for her opposition to Hitler and had spent many months in Nazi prisons, but I did not know it at the time. I had blushed simply because I was ashamed of being accused of hate: so I had explained it to myself. The real truth was different: I had blushed because I was ashamed of having permitted my hate to get away from me. It was this shame that overwhelmed me in Germany: I was betraying the dead. Instead of judging the Germans, then, I judged myself.

After the war, one question had absorbed me: how to explain the absence of an urge to vengeance on the part of the survivors? When Buchenwald was liberated, the Russian prisoners lost no time commandeering American jeeps and driving to Weimar, where for hours on end they machine-gunned inhabitants for having led a normal—if not peaceful—life on the other side of the barbed wire. The liberated Jews did nothing like this. Why not?

In Palestine, in *kibbutzim* and around Palmach campfires, the idea of vengeance was violently argued—and rejected. The basic principle was that Nazi crimes must be opposed by humane justice: hate must not be fought with hate. We had to show the executioners our moral superiority, prove to other peoples that Jews are incapable of deeds of hate. Hatred of the enemy—especially in his defeat—has never been a Jewish habit. "Rejoice not on seeing thine enemy struck down," Solomon teaches.

There is a passage in the *Midrash* which describes the wrath of God against his angels who had begun singing his praises as the Jews were crossing the Red Sea. "My creatures [the Egyptians] are drowning and you are disposed to sing?" And though he lost his throne for it, Saul refused to kill Agag, the Amalekite king who is the symbol of Israel's hereditary enemy. Typically, in the few places where hatred does figure in the Bible, it is always of family, of tribe, or of neighbor—not of foreigners. Jews are suspicious of foreigners, they do not hate them. The Torah bids us remember Amalek, not hate him. In modern times, the ghetto Jews expended upon the *Judenrat* a more concentrated hatred than upon the Germans themselves, and during the British occupation of Palestine, the secret political organizations hated each other more than they hated the English.

The night Eichmann was executed, a friend made a remark which at the time left me perplexed: he could not help feeling a kind of pity for this functionary of death as he stepped to the scaffold. I protested violently. It was, indeed, not until I re-entered Germany that I understood about hate, a hate that was more than desirable: a justified hate. It escapes us, disappears as the events that engendered it have disappeared.

A Jewish poet in an extermination camp prayed: "O God, give me the strength to hate." He had more than enough reasons, it was only strength he lacked. Two thousand years of persecution had failed to prepare the Jewish mentality for hate, had only immunized it against hate. Jewish history is full of examples, from Akiba to Hillel Zeitlin, of how the Jews have always been able to meet beast with man, massacre with prayer, cruelty with faith.

It must be said, moreover, that relations between Jews and Germans—aside from the business of propaganda—had always been, in the time of the apocalypse, devoid of hatred. This seems strange, yet it is what gave—and still gives—the tragedy its true dimension of horror. "I am not an anti-Semite," Eichmann proclaimed in his trial at Jerusalem: the very Eichmann responsible for thousands of death trains. Absurd as it seems, he was probably telling the truth. He killed off Jews—and he did not necessarily hate them. The Nazis saw Jews not as human beings—stimulating hatred or justifying it—but simply as objects, minerals, numbers: one does not hate numbers. As for the

Jews, they saw the Germans as a machine crushing life and spirit, reducing them to ashes: one does not hate a machine.

In the camp—I am trying to remember—my senses were too atrophied to allow me to be capable of hate. Yet if I was able to feel hate, it was directed toward my bunkmate because he had wangled an additional ration of soup or bread. You hate man. For us the SS guards were a force that destroyed and denied man. You do not hate the stone that crushes you, or the animal that devours you. Only man inspires hate, and only man suffers it. At the moment of his death, the victim does not cast his last glance of hate at the executioner: it is his comrades he hates, those who betrayed or abandoned or forgot him, or simply those who will remain alive. The executioner already belongs to the landscape of death. "I forgive you!" Pierre Laval shouted these last words to the soldiers of the firing squad. His hate was directed toward the judges and witnesses, toward the joy of the victors—his equals, whom chance had favored. In our heart of hearts, we hate only what resembles us. The first murder was a fratricide.

There is a time to love and a time to hate; whoever does not hate when he should does not deserve to love when he should, does not deserve to love when he is able. Perhaps, had we learned to hate more during the years of ordeal, fate itself would have taken fright. The Germans did their best to teach us, but we were poor pupils in the discipline of hate. Yet today, even having been deserted by my hate during that fleeting visit to Germany, I cry out with all my heart against silence. Every Jew, somewhere in his being, should set apart a zone of hate—healthy, virile hate—for what the German personifies and for what persists in the German. To do otherwise would be a betrayal of the dead.

I shall not return to Germany soon again.

13.

Moscow Revisited

Actually, I should have been disappointed. I had in fact anticipated a certain letdown, and had even prepared myself for it. No holiday can be real unless it has something of the miraculous about it, and by definition a miracle must be a single, unique event. In this case, I had seen it all the year before: the ecstatic prayers of the Hasidim on the night of Shemini Atzeret; the processions in the Central Synagogue on Simchat Torah; the furtive questions put in a whisper to foreign guests; the communal singing; the sudden appearance of thousands of youngsters, demonstrating in public their unshakable

solidarity with the Jewish people. Such images—sorrow-
ful and sublime at once—had been indelibly engraved
upon my memory from my last visit to Moscow in the fall
of 1965. My experience then had been so strong, and so
deep, that I feared a mere duplication of it would rob
the event of one of its most important dimensions, and
myself of a priceless memory. What would happen this
year had already happened before. It would no longer be
a mystery, or a surprise, but would seem somehow natural and routine. I had already seen everything to be
seen, and had said about it everything I was prepared to
say. There are some visions which I am convinced we
must not behold more than once.

Yet I decided to return. Why, I don't myself know.
Perhaps because I needed to confirm, for myself, that
what I had seen and heard the year before was not in the
nature of a momentary dream that had suddenly ignited
my imagination. Or perhaps I returned because I felt an
inner need to spend this particular holiday with these
particular Jews. Something, at any rate, drew me to them
—to their songs, to their enthusiasm, to their pride. And
once among them, I witnessed a second miracle. Far from
being disappointed, far from having to undergo the mere
repetition of a previous experience, I found myself caught
up in new surprises, and overcome by a new shock of
recognition. The report I brought back last year was true
—that much has not changed; but now I have come to
see that its import is both more valid and more serious
than even I had thought at the time. It may even be for
this new knowledge that I returned.

I arrived in Moscow on October 5, the sixth day of
Sukkot. Upon reaching my hotel I learned that a performance would be given that same evening by one of the
Soviet Union's few troupes of Yiddish actors, led by the
famous singer, Anna Gozik. It is virtually impossible to

get tickets to these programs, even though they always consist of the same play: Sholem Aleichem's *Wandering Stars*—the only offering in the troupe's repertoire. People who have seen the performance twenty times return avidly for a twenty-first; the troupe visits Moscow only once a year, and the theater is always packed.

I noticed in the audience a considerable number of young people, who followed the action of the play through the whispered translations of their parents and grandparents. Whenever an actor delivered a line that suggested a double meaning, the audience burst into applause and loud bravos—as for instance when Miss Gozik, portraying Uriel daCosta, declared, "I am a Jew, and a Jew I shall remain!" The significance of such an affirmation for the Jews of the Soviet Union cannot be overestimated. The musical theme that evening was *Hava Nagilah;* at the end, everyone in the audience sang it together with the cast.

During intermission I spoke with some of the youngsters I had spotted in the audience. Although I asked them dutifully why they had bothered coming to a Yiddish performance rather than attending a Russian play or ballet, I knew beforehand what they would answer. In fact, they will go to anything that is Jewish, and are irrepressibly curious about the fragments which still remain of a Jewish culture that was once quite powerful in their country. Should a Yiddish theater be established again in Moscow, there would be no difficulty filling the auditorium. Of that I am sure.

The next day I went to the Central Synagogue on Arkhipova Street. The sanctuary had been redecorated since the last time I was inside; it seemed better lit, more attractive. By contrast, however, the venerable Chief Rabbi, Yehuda Leib Levin, appeared to have aged. It was clear from the weariness and grief reflected in his dark eyes that he had not yet recovered from the incident that had occurred in his congregation on Yom Kippur, and

about which I had heard the night before. In his sermon
on that day he had spoken in passing of the "two million"
Jews murdered by the Germans twenty-five years before.
A number of those present in the synagogue protested,
"Six million, not two!" The unfortunate rabbi was forced
to explain that he had been referring only to Jews who
were Soviet citizens. Unable—or unwilling—to understand why the rabbi felt constrained to differentiate
among Jews, especially dead Jews, the congregation protested again. One supposes that they were justified in
their complaint, although it is not for us to judge. The
rabbi speaks as he is told to speak, and there is no guaran-
tee that another man would have spoken differently.

The sexton had also changed. He too seemed older, less
sprightly than a year ago. Who knows what he had gone
through since then. Standing some distance from him was
the most notorious of the Moscow "informers," a short
hunchbacked man—wearing a green hat—whose features
bore ugly testimony to his vocation. I myself saw him
strike a Jew who dared to ask me for a prayer shawl and
siddur. It is estimated that there are at least twenty informers in the Moscow congregation—a number large
enough to ensure the perpetuation of a constant sense of
fear and suspicion among the others. It was this sense of
fear that had been most strongly impressed upon me in
my last visit, and that had haunted me throughout the
year.

This time, however, I had come not in order to witness
Jewish fear, but to participate in a Jewish festival. The
following evening was Simchat Torah, the occasion
which tens of thousands of Jewish youngsters have
chosen as their annual evening of public celebration.
During the previous week, posters had appeared on bul-
letin boards around the university: "The 'symphony' of
Simchat Torah will be performed on the night of October

6, as usual, at the usual time and place." On that night, between thirty and forty thousand young Jews appeared outside the Central Synagogue, where they remained almost until dawn, singing and dancing in Hasidic abandon.

By now, this holiday has become something of a tradition in the Soviet Union. The numbers of the participants have steadily increased over the years, and this year—although estimates vary according to the hours at which they were made—there appear to have been close to forty thousand youngsters at the Moscow synagogue. The police closed off the neighboring streets to traffic, and doctors and ambulances were stationed nearby in case of need. They were never called upon. Throughout the entire night of dancing, not a single person was injured; no one fainted, no one needed emergency first-aid. No one became drunk or got out of hand. Not a single person was arrested.

(About two or three years ago, the authorities had in fact tried to discourage similar festivities in Leningrad. The young people were asked to disperse. When they refused, about ten of them were arrested on the spot, but the others simply went on singing as if nothing had happened. Since then, the government has taken a more tolerant position: it allows Jewish youth to have its one holiday a year.)

As the first young people began to gather in the street outside the Moscow synagogue, I sat inside, waiting for the religious ceremonies to begin. Despite the unbearable crowding, the sanctuary seemed to exude a distinct air of lighthearted cheer. No one complained about the need to stand for long periods of time, or about the lack of room. Everyone—men, women, and children—waited patiently for the processions to begin. Of the four generations that had gathered together this evening, only the oldest knew what it was to pray. The oldsters still keep the tradition, while their grandchildren clearly have no concept of

what the Jewish religion entails. They are interested not
so much in the Jewish God, as in the Jewish people. Yet
they too had pushed their way into the synagogue, to see
for themselves what was to transpire in front of the Holy
Ark.

This year, too, the ceremonies began only after a considerable delay. The congregation was not in a hurry.
Friends shook hands, strangers exchanged smiles of greeting. Men and women mixed freely rather than remaining
in their customary separate sections. Tonight, all barriers
had fallen. Tonight it was permissible to talk, to laugh, to
trust in the future. Even to converse with guests from
abroad. Tonight, the hunchbacked informer, his eyes
bulging with the rage of thwarted authority, was powerless.

The time came to begin. The foreign guests were invited to participate in the first procession, which was led
by the Chief Rabbi himself. Each of us took a Torah scroll,
and we set out together on our circuit of the hall. Within
a matter of seconds, we had become separated, each of us
surrounded by a sea of heads. The Jews refused to let us
move. Kissing the Torah I held in my arms, they show-
ered me with blessings and personal requests: "Tell them
in Israel we're with them"; "Be strong, be valiant";
"Don't forget us, we haven't forgotten you." Later I was
to find little slips of paper that had been thrust into my
pockets: "Next year in Jerusalem"; "Blessings from an
old Jew who will die on foreign soil"; a verse from *Hatik-
vah*. One of these pieces of paper had a characteristic request: "Please, give me a Hebrew grammar book for my
son. He wants to learn. I'll wait for you tonight at ten.
Outside." Just like that. No name, no place of meeting.

I tried to move forward, to complete our circuit of the
hall; the procession had lasted a long time. Each step
forward was like crossing the Red Sea. They refused to let
me go. At that moment I had become for them a living
link with world Jewry. Here and there I met persons I

had spoken with the year before. We managed a few
hasty conversations. "Has anything changed?" Nothing.
"Is the situation better?" No. "Worse?" No. Three Jews
had been sentenced to death for "economic crimes." In
one city or another, the warden of a synagogue had been
ordered to sever connections with his co-religionists in
Moscow. "Are you still afraid?" Still. "What will happen?" Hope for the best. . . .

On the dais stood a young man wearing glasses; he was
an army officer, recently discharged. He held in his arms
a Torah scroll which he refused to relinquish. He stood
close to the microphone, and his voice rolled out over the
hall: "Blessed is our God who has created us for his glory
. . . O, O, for his glory." The old rabbi began to sing along
with him: "Yes, Yes . . . for his glory." Hundreds joined
in. Only the sexton seemed serious, abstracted—as if he
had for the first time discovered the meaning of the words
and was quietly taking pity on him who created such a
world for his glory; or perhaps on himself for having
been forced to live in such a world.

Last year, the younger people who came to the synagogue had remained separated from the older Jews. This
year, however, they too took part in the festivities, if only
as enthusiastic onlookers. Here and there one of them
overcame his embarrassment and, following the example
of his neighbors, kissed the Torah (even though no one
ever told him what is written in it), or sang a Hasidic
tune he had just learned (without pronouncing the
words). A girl clapped her hands, another girl grinned
broadly. Behind her stood a boy, preoccupied with his
thoughts. I turned to him: "What are *you* doing here?"
He answered, "No, you tell me." I knew the answer, even
if it had not yet penetrated his own consciousness. He
knew that I knew. He smiled at me: he was looking for
himself.

This boy's education had failed him. He had been
taught to despise his origins—yet he had returned to

them. Every attempt had been made to poison his attitude toward Judaism—yet he had retained his ties. Nothing he had learned in school, or in libraries and youth
clubs, had succeeded in cutting him off from his community. He had been taught that Judaism was an anach-
ronism, that only criminals frequented the synagogue
—yet this too had failed to sway him. He does not, to be
sure, come to the synagogue to pray, but he does come to
see Jews praying. And that is enough. There are certain
silent glances that are worth more than all the prayers
composed by the ancients.

As was the case last year, however, the real holiday did
not take place inside, but outside in front of the synagogue, where two gigantic floodlights had been installed
to illuminate the street. It seemed as if the entire city had
emptied its youngsters here, where now they formed into
groups, singing and dancing. One circle stood around a
girl strumming her guitar and singing Yiddish folktunes.
Further away, hundreds of students listened to a young
man coaxing a melody from his balalaika. There in the
corner someone played a harmonica, and there again I
found an amateur poet reciting satiric verses about anti-
Semitism in Russia. All these voices and melodies seemed
to swell together into one pure crescendo of sound, overwhelming the listener and drawing him inexorably into
the mounting wave of excitement. Last year the youngsters knew only two or three Yiddish and Hebrew songs.
This year they had managed to learn another, and yet
another. But their own unique anthem had not changed.
It is a song we used to sing at Jewish weddings, when
the guests were invited to greet the bride and groom; but
the lyrics have been altered by these youngsters so as to
refer to their new-found identity: "Come let us go, all of
us together, and greet the people Israel."

Walking among them, I suddenly recalled a story by I.
L. Peretz about a village lad who played his flute in the
synagogue because he didn't know how to pray. Like

him, these youngsters also do not know how to pray—nor, perhaps, are they interested in prayer. But they know how to sing, and how to dance. And as a Hasidic Rebbe once put it, it is also possible to bring the Messiah through the power of dance.

At a certain moment, close to midnight, the lights went out. The two floodlights in front of the synagogue suddenly went dark and stood like blind men. A gloom descended over Arkhipova Street. The crowd stood silent, confused, waiting. Short circuit? No. A subtle hint from above that it was time to break up. One mustn't overdo things. Tomorrow was a schoolday, a workday. It was time to stop, time to go home for another long year. One could return in 1967.

The confusion lasted no more than a minute. It was followed by a groan of disappointment, then a roar of protest. They didn't want to leave. Somebody took a newspaper out of his pocket and set it on fire—the natural act of a man who wished to see where he was. His neighbors quickly followed suit. The idea seemed to please everyone, and word of it was passed along from group to group, from circle to circle. Thousands of newspapers were lit at once, and within a matter of moments the celebration had become transformed into a weird procession of people bearing flaming torches. No one organized this parade, no one arranged for it ahead of time. No one could even have known it would take place. It all happened quite suddenly, and in silence. The quiet was virtually absolute. There was no singing, no talking—only the crackle of burning paper.

Then, in the quiet, about a hundred students climbed onto the balcony of a nearby building. Holding their torches high, they began to chant in unison in both Hebrew and Russian: "The people Israel lives! The people Israel lives! The people Israel lives!" The slogan electri-

fied those standing below, and they roared in answer:
"Hurrah! Hurrah! Hurrah!" It was a simple and spontaneous affirmation, but one which should put to rest our
doubts about the future of Jewish youth in Russia. There,
too, the people Israel lives.

This, perhaps, is the most forceful lesson now to be
learned about the Jews of the Soviet Union. Although the
same evening had made an overwhelming impression
upon me a year ago as well, this time the experience was
deeper, and more complete. It had taken on a new and all-
important dimension of self-assurance. Not only were
more young people present, but they had given a more
open and straightforward expression to their Jewishness.
It is a mistake to speak of this event as a passing phenomenon; those who are still accustomed to declare at every
opportunity that in the course of ten years there will be
not a single trace left of Jewish life in Soviet Russia have
not seen these youngsters. It is true, of course, that in the
past, certain activities took place only in darkness. Young
people preferred to meet in the shadows, in side-street
courtyards. Unsure of themselves, they could hardly become reconciled to the fact that someone had taken the
initiative of setting up special floodlights in the street
for the holiday. Despite the general easing of tensions,
they remained, justifiably, suspicious. There was no way
of knowing whether the man standing off at the side,
watching the celebration, was not memorizing names or
faces.

This year, however, they had taken the decisive step:
they became angry when the lights went out. Now they
were demanding both to see and to be seen. For me, their
spontaneous torchlight parade is a symbol of their new
desire to come up from underground, and to assert their
Jewishness in open pride.

On this visit, too, I talked with them for long hours on

end. Their knowledge of Jewish matters has not im-
proved. Their faith in Marxism has not been shaken, nor
have their ties to Soviet Russia been weakened. I heard
not a single word of criticism against the regime in which
they live. But I can report that their Jewish consciousness
has taken deeper root. Judaism is no longer a matter of
apologetics with them. Unlike many of their counterparts
in the West, they are not defensive about their Jewishness, but regard it as a basic fact of life which is not open
to discussion or philosophical debate.

"Anyone who wants to defame us can go ahead and do
so," said a chemistry student I had talked to once before, a
year ago. "That's their business. We simply don't answer.
We refuse to argue with them. Our answer lies in the fact
that we continue to survive—and that we wish to go on
surviving."

Another student said, "We refuse to lower ourselves to
their level. They've convinced us we're right, and that's
the greatest compliment we can pay them."

A girl, a student of Western literature and a friend of
them both, said to me in Yiddish: "No one denies that
there are anti-Semites here. We present a problem to
them, but we've decided not to let them present a problem to us. Once and for all, we've simply refused."

And yet, it is the anti-Semites who have caused these
youngsters to return to Judaism, who have coerced them
into becoming more Jewish. "It hurts me that our 'revival'
has come about because of external, rather than internal,
pressures; my only comfort is that this fact hurts the anti-
Semites even more," said a man who teaches foreign languages at one of the Soviet universities. A year ago this
same man had told me how he had decided not to tell his
son about his annual visits to Arkhipova Street, on the
night of Simchat Torah, but had then actually met his son
here, in the crowd. "This year we came together," he said
proudly. I asked him about the rest of the year. Did he
talk with his son about Jewish matters? No. His wife is

not Jewish, he explained, and there seems no reason to cause trouble at home. "But," he went on, "let's not worry. The situation cannot remain static. It has to change. Once you come to dance on Simchat Torah, you want to live like a Jew the rest of the year too. We'll see."

Indeed, since last year the situation has clearly changed. Young people who formerly knew about the existence of one Jewish holiday have uncovered others. Rosh Hashana and Yom Kippur do not, it is true, attract them; they want to celebrate, not to fast and grieve. The "festival of freedom" is a far more exciting prospect. On a night during Passover 1966, several hundred youngsters gathered opposite the Moscow synagogue and began to dance and sing. They were the pioneer core, scouting the territory. Had there been no interference, Passover would probably have become another Simchat Torah. Someone, however, suggested to the community leaders that it was inadvisable to overdo such things. The warden of the synagogue was sent outside to ask them to leave. When this failed, the old rabbi himself came out and begged them to return home. "You're disturbing the peace," he told them. The youngsters finally took pity on these men, and rather than endanger their position with the authorities, decided to leave. They could wait until October. On Simchat Torah all the enthusiasm pent up during the year would finally be released.

About a thousand men and women filled the synagogue on the following day, for the second ceremony of processions. Many had brought presents for the guests: vodka, cake, and apples. They had saved up for a week or a month in order to provide this personal gift to the Jews who came to them from afar. A bottle of liquor costs about five rubles—a day's wages for an officeworker or skilled laborer. I found myself surrounded by a dozen men, all pleading with me to drink, to accept a piece of cake or an apple. The congregation consists in the main of *pensionnaires,* retired workers. Last night was the youngsters' holiday; today was theirs. "Drink *lehayyim,*" a Jew whispered to me. "I've kept this bottle for six months, waiting for this moment." Standing next to him was a man with a red beard, who also urged me to drink: "Drink to us all; who knows, maybe your benedictions will be accepted in heaven."

Here and there I heard people say proudly that the whole city was talking about what had happened the night before. Thirty to forty thousand youngsters had taken part in the "symphony of Simchat Torah," and no one had been arrested, or even molested. This morning the chief trustee had contacted the police to ask if everything had been all right. Everything was fine. Not a single incident had been reported—highly unusual in the case of such a large gathering.

The processions ended. Men were being called up to the Torah. We all sang: "Blessed be he who has chosen us from among all nations and given us his Torah." I returned to my bench in the visitors' loge. Hunched in a corner, I read the anonymous notes I had once again found in my pocket: "Next year in Jerusalem"; "Be strong and valiant"; "Don't forget us. . . ."

Suddenly, to my astonishment, I heard singing outside. I thought at first it was the effect of the vodka. But the voices became louder. I left the visitors' section and hurried out to the street. I couldn't believe my eyes. Hundreds of young Jews were there, singing and dancing, exactly like the night before. Where they had come from, how they had managed to leave their classrooms or offices —I don't know. But they had come. Once again the police were called upon to block the street off. Only pedestrians were allowed to pass, and I heard some of them querying the officers about what was going on. One of the policemen replied, "It's just the Jews, celebrating their holiday."

For the second time in twenty-four hours I heard the

old familiar songs in Yiddish and Russian. Circles were
again formed to dance the *hora*. A young man climbed on
the shoulders of his friends, shouting, "Long live the
Jewish people!" The crowd roared back its approval, and
urged him on. For a minute he seemed at a loss, then recovered himself and began to shout out the names of
famous Jewish personalities in the Soviet Union: "Long
live Benjamin Dimshitz!" "Long live David Oistrakh!"
"Leonid Kogan!" "Yevsei Liberman!" "Botvinik!" "Maya
Plisetskaya!" "Nehama Lipshitz!" All Jews. But the list
was quickly exhausted and his audience wanted more. Un-
thinking, he chose the name of one long forgotten: "Long
live Lazar Kaganovitch!" Someone near me asked jok-
ingly whether Kaganovitch was still alive. Yes, he is still
alive, but only the Jews remember him. I wonder if it
ever crossed his mind that a day would come when his
name would be trumpeted aloud outside the Jewish synagogue, while he himself was banished from the Kremlin
walls.

A boy was pointed out to me who had traveled a distance of thirty miles in order to return a notebook that
belonged to a foreign tourist. A second had come all the
way from the other end of Moscow because the night
before someone had promised to bring him a Hebrew
calendar. Others came for no specific reason other than to
continue what had been started the night before, as if
they had simply resolved to ignore their official allotment
of one night a year. It appears that when I expected to
see nothing new here this year, I too had not reckoned
with Jewish youth.

In all other areas, however, it must be said that the
situation remains as petrified as ever. No one holds out
any hope that the general discriminatory measures
against Jews will be put to an end. German citizens living
in the Soviet Union, for instance, have their own schools,

their own theater, their own folklore, publishing houses, cultural life, and even radio and television programs. The Jews still have nothing. All others can pride themselves on their national heritage—but not the Jews.

As for the economic trials, it is difficult to ascertain whether they have been completely stopped or not. The press, at any rate, has ceased to publicize them, and that is a good sign. But there are persistent rumors about Jews who have been sentenced to death or imprisonment for alleged economic crimes. These rumors are not spontaneous, nor are they groundless: the place of trial and the names of the accused are known. In addition, the pervasive fear which I encountered a year ago may still be said to exist. This time, too, I came across Jewish tourists from abroad who had tried unsuccessfully to speak with their relatives in Kiev and Minsk. The average Russian citizen does not hesitate to talk with foreigners; Jews shy away from them. In the synagogue I met someone who had been interrogated about a conversation he had had with me last year. They had showed him photographs, had wanted to know every question I asked him and what he had replied. He was released after twenty-four hours, but the effects of the interrogation had yet to wear off. Only because there was a large crowd around us did he feel free to speak with me again. In another place, in different circumstances, he would have avoided me completely. He told me so himself.

On the other hand, I heard of Jews in other cities who had overcome their fear. This year a number of Jews even had the courage to request permission to be reunited with their families abroad. A short while ago an old Hasid was granted an exit visa. Hundreds of his fellow Hasidim, singing and dancing, accompanied him to the train station, to the general astonishment of the other passengers. No one interfered.

Whether or not there will be interference in the future, only time can tell. I believe, however, that no amount of interference will succeed in dampening the new spirit of awakening that breathes in Soviet Jewry, especially among the young. And I believe that the authorities know this. Soviet policy toward the Jews seems to be at a crossroads; the trouble is that no matter which direction it finally takes, the results will in all likelihood be the same. A policy of leniency—even token leniency—will cause many Jews who have hitherto wandered about as strangers among strangers, along the fringes of their people, to return to Judaism. Once it is known that it is permissible to live openly as a Jew—without the fear of public insults and degradation—such people will return in the thousands, for the simple reason that it has been proved to them in their very bones that a Jew cannot live in Russia as a non-Jew.

But an opposite policy—of suppression through the real means of fear and terrorization—will only bring about similar results. The experience of past years has taught us that young Jews will oppose this kind of pressure. They have already demonstrated their unwillingness to surrender either to blandishments or to threats, and their adherence to Judaism will increase precisely as they are asked to reject it. The further they are separated from their people, the more will they assert their identification with it.

It is possible therefore to say that Soviet authorities have missed their opportunity. It may be that at one time —two or three generations ago—it was possible to solve the "Jewish problem" in the Soviet Union, for better or for worse, through a process of voluntary or forced assimilation. Many Jews, if given the opportunity, would perhaps have tried to assimilate and to live as non-Jews; but this was denied them. The general populace refused to accept them as citizens with equal rights. A Jew born as a Jew remained a Jew until the day of his death, whether he liked it or not. His national origin was stamped on all his documents.

By now, however, young Jews in Russia have rejected the solution of assimilation altogether. Although they have had no education in Judaism—except what they have learned from anti-Semitic literature—they cling ferociously to their community. Although non-religious, they celebrate Jewish holidays and sing Jewish songs. Under no circumstances will they allow their Jewishness to be degraded or killed.

I returned from my second trip to Moscow somewhat encouraged. I am convinced that however events turn out, these young Jews will continue to seize every available opportunity to demonstrate their solidarity with the Jewish community. I have no doubt that in the not too distant future they will appear in front of the synagogue not just once a year but twice, then three or four times, and then once a month. Something is taking place among Jewish youth in the Soviet Union, and the time has come for us to realize it. Without outside help, without teachers or books, without leaders and meeting places, even without an appropriate spiritual climate, they have managed to survive, and will manage in the future as well. And they will do so, I should add, on their own. They learn Hebrew in secret, translate a Hebrew song into Russian, pass from hand to hand slips of paper with a few lines of Jewish history written on them. They listen to foreign broadcasts and circulate among themselves news of what is happening in world Jewry and in the Jewish state. This activity is not organized by any single person in any single place. Each one of them takes part and feels personally responsible for its success.

Their salvation, then, will come from within themselves, not from us. They may already have realized how futile it is to rely on us—either on our help or on our sympathy—and so have taken their destiny into their own hands. In past years, guests from abroad played an important role on the night of Simchat Torah. Each one of us would be surrounded by hundreds of youngsters, and we would tell them what was happening elsewhere in the world. We taught them new songs. This time, however, we were only observers. A year ago, they seemed to be making a conscious effort to explain and clarify their Jewishness, both for themselves and for others. This year, everything had suddenly become clear. Few of the participants were to be seen engaged in discussions among themselves or with the foreign guests. Rather than besiege us with questions, they appeared content with what they themselves knew. They didn't need us any longer. And the next day, when they came in groups to the synagogue, and began to sing and dance, it was without our knowledge. We went home; they continued to dance and shout: "The people Israel lives!" That song will never die.

14.
The Guilt We Share

The trial of Eichmann at Jerusalem may be called historic insofar as it aimed not merely at judging the crimes and moral degradation of a single individual—or even of a system—but at trying to define more clearly a whole epoch of our history. That epoch, up to now, has eluded all human understanding—so inhumanly blind were its drives, so terrible their consequences.

Not one, but two peoples were transformed: the one into the murderers, the other into the silent horde of the murdered. How was it possible? we still ask sixteen years later. How was an Eichmann possible? We ask the question in anguish—we are in the dark, still. How explain away so total a triumph of beastliness over man, and at the expense of the destruction of a whole people? How, and why? At a certain point in the asking, the why and the how come together, indistinguishably.

Those of us who looked to the trial for an answer to these questions looked in vain. I asked Alfred Kazin one day if he thought the death of six million Jews could have any meaning; and he replied that he hoped not. There can, indeed, be no answer naked enough, or real enough. But the trial should at the very least have shaped the question, should at least have revealed the cry inside the question that will echo through all time. Simply to condemn Eichmann was not enough; not even, in fact, possible. The enormity, call it even the absurdity, of his acts, transcended his person and placed him outside of temporal justice. The laws of living men could not judge him—only the dead could confront him. It was this that often made the trial seem unreal: that the principal characters, Eichmann foremost, appeared actually to be at ease in their respective roles, as if they had come together in the usual kind of judicial proceeding, the ordinary sort of trial where a man is being judged by his peers. Not so: not he, not Eichmann was being tried, but History. The accused Eichmann spoke freely, unafraid. He cited documents and figures, he held back nothing—he was desperately bent on saving his neck. Thus he often succeeded in giving a false emphasis to the proceedings. Yet we all know that it was not Eichmann's neck that was really at stake. The case of Eichmann—symbol as well as individual—had to be judged in the domain of psychiatry and metaphysics, and not only by the processes of law.

It was precisely this kind of larger scope that the trial never achieved, as critics of the proceedings have pointed out. The beam of light that it threw did not encompass enough and therefore failed to uncover all the dark horizons. And if the focus of the trial was too narrow, the reason was that the proceedings got stuck inside the rules of the legal game. The accused should have constituted the point of departure—he was, instead, the end in sight. So the equation was necessarily falsified: if, before the law, the Eichmanns are guilty, the others, therefore, are innocent. But the truth leads to a different conclusion: the others are guilty, too.

All of us, I believe, in varying degrees must take responsibility for what happened in Europe—Curzio Malaparte and even Karl Jaspers have pointed this out. We belong to a generation at once lost and guilty, and our collective conscience lies under a weight of humiliation. It is too easy to put the whole brunt on a single Eichmann: to do so is to evade coming face to face with the problem. No one ever doubted Eichmann's guilt; everyone was convinced of it from the start, and no trial was needed for proof. If the trial was important—and I for one believe it was—it was because by reviving the past it was able to demonstrate how a crime could spill over and outward, and splash its guilt onto those who thought themselves to be standing at a safe distance. If the grandiose proceedings had failed to teach this lesson, they would have been not useless, but incomplete.

Future historians will find plenty of gaps in the Eichmann trial: the research will have to go on. Contrary to what we had every right to expect, the brief of particulars kept within the narrow concerns of the accused, of him who was actually standing trial. The role played in the annihilation program by all humanity—Nazified or otherwise—was brought up only in passing.

Yet, we all know that the Germans could never have succeeded in solving the Jewish Question with such speed and efficiency if it had not been for the help and tacit consent of the Ukrainians, Slovaks, Poles, Hungarians. The Slovaks paid for every person the Germans took out of their country; the Hungarians put pressure on Eichmann—who was by no means lacking in enthusiasm himself—to speed up the transports; the Letts and Ukrainians in their cruelty surpassed the Germans themselves; and as for the Poles, it was not by accident that the worst concentration camps were set up in Poland, worse than anywhere else.

But it is a well-established fact that wherever the local population was opposed to the deportation of their Jewish fellow citizens, the "yield" was poor—unsatisfactory to the Nazis. Eichmann himself emphasized this point in the confessions he made to the journalist Wilhelm Sassen, at Buenos Aires. In Denmark, almost the total Jewish population was saved. And because the Nazis could not get wide support for their anti-Jewish measures from the people of France, Belgium, or Holland, Eichmann's henchmen did not do very well in those countries either —to the bitter disgust of the authorities at Berlin, it is known. Only where the indigenous populations were themselves eager to become *Judenrein* did the cattle trains with their suffocating human cargo roll swiftly into the night. This very important fact was hardly touched on at the Jerusalem trial.

Nor did the indictment at Jerusalem dwell much on the failure of the whole outside world, which looked on in a kind of paralysis and passively allowed whatever was being done to be done. The number—six million Jews murdered—could never have been reached if the voices of Roosevelt, Churchill, and the Pope had been more distinctly heard. If the Germans took the precautions they did to cover up their bloody deeds, it was because they were not indifferent to world opinion. In the confessions at Buenos Aires which I cited above, Eichmann notes— with amusement—that even if, through Joel Brand, he had managed to put up a million Jews for sale, there was not a single country which would have bought them. The indifference of our civilized world allowed the Germans a free hand: go ahead, do what seems best to you with your Jews, we see nothing.

By 1942, Washington, London, and, yes, Jerusalem, too, were aware of what was going on, and Hitler and Goebbels on their side were expecting an avalanche of angry protestations. When none came, they understood: they had been given a free hand by the Western powers.

In the Jerusalem courtroom, correspondence between Chaim Weizmann and the British Foreign Office was offered in evidence: it spoke of a simple, touching favor that Weizmann had asked for: would His Majesty's government give the order to the Royal Air Force to bomb the railway tracks to Auschwitz? The answer was no. It is known that a similar request was addressed to President Roosevelt by one of the American Jewish leaders who had an entrée to the White House. As we also know, Roosevelt did nothing about it.

Is it not strange—let us use only that word—that the civilized world waited until it was too late before expressing its moral indignation, waited until there were scarcely any Jews left to be saved?

And finally, in order to keep inviolate the historical truth, the prosecutor should have removed the last taboo: to reveal the sorry but nonetheless ineluctable fact that the Jews themselves failed to do everything they should have done: they ought to have done more, they could have done better. The American Jewish community never made adequate use of its political and financial powers; certainly it did not move heaven and earth, as it should have. We know the reasons and the justifications: they are not good enough. There can be no justification, nor any explanation for passivity when an effort had to be made to save five to ten thousand Jews from murder each day. Just how many meetings were there at Madison Square Garden, and how many demonstrations in front of the White House? To think of how few makes one's blood run cold.

In Palestine, the situation was hardly different. In Palestine, heart and conscience of the Jewish people, the means had not yet been found as late as the end of 1944 to give warning, or help if necessary, to the dense centers of Europe's Jewish populations, over which death already hovered. By the time the few parachutists had landed in Budapest (with what results we learned from the Kastner trial) there was nothing they could do: half of Europe had been emptied of Jews. Why had agents not been sent over from Palestine sooner, with or without parachutists' uniforms? Yes, we know that there was the war in Palestine, but the young men of Palmach would gladly have volunteered to go. Ten, maybe only five, out of a hundred volunteers might have reached their destination in Europe; even those ten or five could have organized resistance, escape, rescues.

One of the war's most unforgivable incidents occurred when the Hungarian Jews from Transylvania were deported to Auschwitz. Their mass deportation took place in May–June of 1944, just a few days before the landing at Normandy. Arriving at the Auschwitz station, they still had no idea of what lay in wait for them; they were ignorant of the very name of the place, they had not heard of the horrors it concealed from them. Had they known, they could have made a dash for it, been saved. Not all, maybe, but the great majority. Mountains surrounded the area, and the Jews might have fled into these mountains and hidden out for a while. The Red Army had advanced to within eighteen to twenty miles from Auschwitz, and at night the rumbling of their guns could be distinctly heard. It was only a matter of a few days before the liberators would appear. But these pious Jews of Transylvania were told that they had nothing to fear, that they were only being transferred further inland—were told and believed, for there was no one to tell them anything else.

This took place, I repeat, in the spring of 1944, by the time every child in Brooklyn, in Whitechapel, and in Tel Aviv knew that Treblinka and Birkenau were something other than the names of provincial little railway stations.

And yet to Joel Brand's urgent solicitation for an interview so that he might make known his doubly tragic mission, Chaim Weizmann replied, through his secretary, that he was at the moment too busy to see Brand, that he would be able to receive him in a couple of weeks. Brand had made it clear, in his letter to Weizmann, that every hour counted; every passing day meant the lives of at least ten thousand Jews. How did Brand not go stark raving mad? That in itself remains, for me, one of the great enigmas—the enigma of man's will to survive his damnation.

The terrible fact is that Weizmann's response reflected an attitude widespread among the Jews of Palestine. An attitude, I dare to say, of an inconceivable detachment. People in Palestine behaved as if what was happening *over there* did not concern them too much. In his memoirs, Yitzchak Grunebaum, who was at one time head of a Rescue Commission, tells how the question came up again and again among his colleagues of whether they had the right, in order to try to save European Jews, to use money earmarked for the building up of Palestine. Grunebaum himself thought absolutely not: first came the Land of Israel, then the Diaspora. The Yishuv's houses, factories, schools, must take priority.

One afternoon during the trial of Eichmann, a young Israeli poet, Haim Gouri, left the courthouse on an impulse. He went to the archives to look through the old Tel Aviv newspapers of 1943-1944. He came back shocked. "I don't understand," he said to me. "If you knew the things that were bothering us here, while *that* was going on in Europe. . . . Front page headlines: Municipal elections at

Hedera—or some other place. . . . And stuck away in a corner of an inside page, an item of a couple of lines: The Germans have begun the extermination of the Jews in the Ghetto of Lublin, or Lodz. . . ."

It was of course not the people's fault, but the fault of their leaders who evinced a surprising lack of initiative, of political maturity, and of courage. Nahum Goldmann acknowledged as much not long ago during a meeting in Geneva of the Executive Committee of the World Jewish Congress. The major Jewish organizations seemed incapable of surmounting their internal bickerings in order to achieve unity of action. The Emergency Committee to Save the Jewish People during the entire time it existed was boycotted by U.S. Jewish leaders. But if these leaders had their good reasons for not wishing to collaborate with this one or that one on the outside—and I daresay they did have their good reasons—why didn't they set up their own Committee of Rescue, one which could represent all the organizations? This they did not do.

Therefore, it seems to me, for the trial to have been conducted on its right moral plane—the plane of absolute truth—the prosecutor, Gideon Hausner (or Ben Gurion himself as witness), should have bowed his head and cried out in a voice loud enough to be heard by three generations: Before judging others, let us look into our own errors, our own weaknesses. We never attempted the impossible—we never even exhausted the possible.

It might be said that with the advent of the Nazi regime in Germany, humanity became witness to what Martin Buber would call an eclipse of God. As if from a mighty curse, strong men and weak men, cowards and those who had been wont to see clearly, were to find themselves guilty in an association with Evil, if from no other cause than that they were living inside the same moment in history. All actions became sullied. Generous spirits fell asleep, distinguished sensibilities were dulled, powerful voices were silenced. The general apathy created the climate in which the criminals on all sides could proceed quietly and efficiently, without disturbance of any kind, and without affected shame.

When the German surrender came, the civilized world uttered a great cry of horror but still shrank from coming to any closer grips with the problem. It wasn't I : this was the popular refrain, and especially in what had been the Third Reich. Elsewhere, people were content to shed a tear, and declare, "We had nothing to do with it."

To be sure, Karl Jaspers set himself the task of investigating the "German guilt," but with the specific intention of thereby demonstrating the universal guilt. As a result, his investigation succeeded in allaying many fears in occupied Germany, in reassuring many uneasy minds. Did this not show, on the part of the German philosopher, a flagrant lack of humility? The non-Nazi world had to be allotted its share of the guilt—but this should have been the task and the duty of the intellectuals of New York or of Stockholm. The world, indeed, had more than a few lessons to learn—but not from a German professor.

In Western Europe, the reaction was to be found mainly in works of literature. Sartre, Camus, Gabriel Marcel, going to Malraux for their theme, stressed action and commitment: everything which happens around us, they proclaimed, involves us directly and necessarily. Yet, in these writings, the question was still not probed deeply enough. The hero of the modern novel, absorbed in expressing his protest, overlooks the nuances. A man was good or bad, a resister or a collaborator, or indifferent. The lines were drawn, the camps strictly defined. Whoever had blown up a train could sleep the sleep of the just, or of the proud, or of the happy. The others were, in this degree or that, vile, *salaud*. The sense of guilt played very little part in the determination of the European youth to build a new future out of the ruins around them. The arts—with the exception of painting—seemed to

have hardly any interior connection with the terrible
events which should have furnished their inspiration. No
new philosophy was engendered, nor any new religion:
the earth had trembled and men had stayed the same.

It is reported that André Gide once told an anti-Semitic
story. And when one of his disciples, blushing, reproached him: "You, too, Master?"—Gide started to cry.
"I did not know that I was," he said. That was before the
war. Afterward, Gide did not cry. He had given up being
witty at the expense of the Jews, so he no longer needed
to feel guilty.

It is by a strange irony of fate that the only ones who
were, who still are, fully conscious of their share of responsibility for the dead are those who were saved, the
ghosts who returned from the dead. They do not feel this
through any concept of original sin; they are Jews, they
do not believe in original sin. The idea that rules them is
more immediate, more agonizing, a part of their very
being.

Why did you not revolt? Why did you not resist? You
were a thousand against ten, against one. Why did you let
yourselves, like cattle, be led to the slaughter?

Well-known psychiatrists have attempted to give some
explanation in their books dealing with the psychology
of the concentration camp. The mystery of the victim's
acceptance occupies them as much as the question of the
executioner's cruelty. But to attribute that acceptance
—as they do—to the disintegration of the personality,
or to the rising up of the "death wish," or to something in Jewish tradition, can only be a partial explanation. The metaphysical *why* is still lacking. Nor is
any account taken of the kind of guilt which had been
implanted in the prisoners.

The feeling of guilt was, to begin with, essentially a
religious feeling. If I am here, it is because God is punish-

ing me; I have sinned, and I am expiating my sins. I have
deserved this punishment that I am suffering. The revolt
against God comes later—it is the final stage. First, the
prisoner sacrifices his own freedom for God's. He prefers
to believe himself guilty rather than think that his God is
the God of Job, for whom man is a mere example—a
means of demonstrating a thesis in a verbal duel with
Satan.

As each passing day took him further and further away
from his freedom, the prisoner's sense of guilt sharpened,
pressed closer on his conscience. He was, in fact, only
following a line of reaction which had been drawn for
him by his jailers who, in the ghettos and in the camps,
had known precisely—shrewdly—how to push to its extreme limit the emotion of shame and humiliation which
he who is still alive normally experiences toward the
dead.

I am alive, therefore I am guilty. If I am still here, it is
because a friend, a comrade, a stranger, died in my place.
Within a closed world, this certitude has a destructive
power whose effects are easy to imagine. If to live means
to accept or engender injustice, to die quickly becomes a
promise and a deliverance.

The system of *Lebensschein* in the ghettos and of
Selekzion in the camps not only periodically decimated
the populations, but also worked on each prisoner to say
to himself: "That could have been me, I am the cause,
perhaps the condition, of someone else's death."

In this way the *Lebensschein* came to stand for a moral
torture . . . a prison without exits. One of the witnesses at
the trial was a man who had been a doctor in Vilna, and
his testimony was terribly moving. Recently married, he
had succeeded in obtaining a "living permit" and was
working in a German factory. He was told he could save
one close relative, and he went to his mother to ask her:
"What shall I do? Whom shall I save? You—or my wife?"
A man forced to make such a choice, to become a con-

crete instrument of destiny, thereafter lives in a suffocating circle of hell; and whenever his thoughts turn to himself, it is in anger and in disgust. If André Schwarz-Bart's hero, Ernie Levy, finally decided to take the train for Auschwitz, it was neither out of love, nor out of pity, but from the conviction that humanity had come to such a pass of evil that no one could continue to live who wished to remain just.

Reduced to a mere number, the man in the concentration camp at the same time lost his identity and his individual destiny. He came to realize that his presence in the camp was due solely to the fact that he was part of a forgotten and condemned collectivity. It is not written: I shall live or die, but: *someone*—today—will vanish, or will continue to suffer; and from the point of view of the collective, it makes no difference whether that someone is I or another. Only the number, only the quota counts. Thus, the one who had been spared, above all during the selections, could not repress his first spontaneous reflex of joy. A moment, a week, or an eternity later, this joy weighted with fear and anxiety will turn into guilt. *I am happy to have escaped death* becomes equivalent to admitting: *I am glad that someone else went in my place.* It was in order not to think about this that the prisoners so very quickly managed to forget their comrades or their relatives: those who had been selected. They forgot them quickly—trying to shut their eyes to the reproachful glances which still floated in the air around them.

Why did the Jews in the camps not choose a death with honor, knife in hand and hate on their lips? It is understandable that all of us should wonder why. Putting aside the technical and psychological reasons which made any attempt at revolt impossible (the Jews knew that they had been sacrificed, forgotten, crossed off by humanity), to answer we must consider the moral aspects of the question. The Jews, conscious of the curse weighing them down, came to believe that they were neither worthy nor capable of an act of honor. To die struggling would have meant a betrayal of those who had gone to their death submissive and silent. The only way was to follow in their footsteps, die their kind of death—only then could the living make their peace with those who had already gone.

There comes to mind another case, also presented before the court at Jerusalem: the case of the woman who, naked and wounded, had managed to escape from the ditch, the mass grave in which all the Jews of her town were mowed down by German machine-guns. That woman returned to the ditch after a little while to rejoin the phantasmagoric community of corpses. Miraculously saved, she still could not accept a life which in her eyes had become impure.

It is not known yet what the psychiatrists uncovered who examined Adolf Eichmann at great length, before and after his trial. Surely Eichmann's victims—those who are alive, that is—ought to be examined. Only, these ghosts maintain against us an oppressive silence which they brought back with them from over there. They refuse to open up. One thing that is not known is that they are afraid of their own voices. Their tragedy is the tragedy of Job before his submission: they believe themselves to be guilty, though they are not. Only a Great Judge would have it in his power to rid them of this burden. But in their eyes no one possesses either such authority or such power: no one, either human or divine.

Therefore they prefer, in this condemned world, not to hurl their defiance at men and their anger into the face of history, but to keep silent, to pursue the monologue which only the dead deserve to hear. Guilt was not invented at Auschwitz, it was disfigured there.

15.
A Plea for the Dead

I was not quite fifteen when, for the first time, completely fascinated, I was present at a strange discussion about dignity and death and the possible relationship between the two.

People who were dead and did not know it yet were discussing the necessity, rather than the possibility, of meeting death with dignity.

The reality of certain words escaped me and the weight of that reality as well. The people around me were talking and I did not understand.

Now, I am more than twenty years older, and all paths

leading to the cemetery are known to me. The discussion
still goes on. Only the participants have changed. Those
of twenty years ago have died and they know it now. As
for me, I understand even less than before.

I had just stepped off into unreality. It must have been
about midnight. Later, I learned that executioners are
usually romantic types who like perfect productions: they
find in darkness a stage setting and in night an ally.

Somewhere a dog began to howl, another echoed him,
then a third. We were, it seemed, in the kingdom of dogs.
One of the women went mad and let out a cry that no
longer resembled anything human; it was more like bark-
ing; no doubt she wanted to become a dog herself. A
pistol shot put an end to her hallucination; silence fell
over us again. In the distance, red and yellow billows of
fire, spewed out by immense smoke-stacks, rose toward
the moonless sky, as if to set it aflame. A quarter of an
hour before, or less, our train had stopped at a small sub-
urban station. Standing at the grates, people read the
name aloud: *Auschwitz.*

Someone asked: "We've arrived?"

Another answered: "I think so."

"Auschwitz, you know it?"

"No. Not at all."

The name evoked no memory, linked itself to no anguish. Ignorant in matters of geography, we supposed it
was a small peaceful spot somewhere in Silesia. We did
not yet know it had already made history with its populace of several million dead Jews. We learned it one
minute later, when the train doors opened into an ear-
splitting din and when an army of inmates began to
shout: "Last stop! Everybody off!"

Like conscientious tour guides, they described the surprises in store for us: "You're acquainted with Auschwitz? You're not? Too bad, you'll get to know it, it won't
be long before you know it."

They sneered: "Auschwitz, you don't know Auschwitz?

Really not? Too bad. Someone is waiting for you here.
Who? Why, death, of course. Death is waiting for you. It
waits only for you. Look and you will see."

And they pointed to the fire in the distance.

Later, many years later, I asked one of my friends:
"What were your first impressions of Auschwitz?"

Somber, he answered me: "I found it a spectacle of
terrifying beauty."

I found it neither beautiful nor terrifying. I was young
and I simply refused to believe my eyes and ears. I
thought: our guides are mocking us in order to scare us.
It amuses them. We are living in the twentieth century,
after all; Jews are not burned anymore. The civilized
world would not allow it. My father walked alongside me,
on my left, his head bowed. I asked him: "The Middle
Ages are behind us, aren't they, Father, far behind us?"

He did not answer me.

I asked him: "I'm dreaming, Father. Am I not dreaming?"

He did not answer me.

We kept moving on toward the unknown. It was then,
like a whisper, a feverish discussion went through the
ranks. Some youths overcoming their stupor, grasping at
their anger, called for a revolt. Without arms? Yes, without arms. Fingernails, fists, and a few penknives hidden in
their clothes, that will suffice. But won't that mean certain death? Yes, so what? There is nothing more to lose
and everything to gain, especially honor, that can still be
gained, honor. To die as free men: that is what they
advocated, those youths. There is defeat only in resignation.

But their fathers were opposed. They went on dreaming. And waiting. They invoked the Talmud: "God can
intervene, even at the very last moment, when everything
seems lost. We must not rush things, we must not lose
faith or hope."

The argument won everyone over. I asked my father: "What do you think?"

This time he did answer me: "Thinking isn't much use anymore."

The human herd marched ahead, we did not know where our steps were leading us. No: we knew, our guides had told us. But we pretended not to know. And the discussions continued. The young were in favor of rebellion, their elders against. The former finally conceded, one must obey one's parents, the Bible says; their wishes must be respected.

And so the revolt did not take place.

In recent times, many people are beginning to raise questions about the problem of the incomprehensible if not enigmatic behavior of Jews in what was concentration-camp Europe. Why did they march into the night the way cattle go to the slaughterhouse? Important, if not essential, for it touches on timeless truth; this question torments men of good conscience who feel the need to be quickly reassured, to have the guilty parties named and their crimes defined, to have unraveled for them the meaning of a history which they have not experienced except through intermediaries. And so those millions of Jews, whom so-called civilized society had abandoned to despair and to agonize in silence and then in oblivion, suddenly are all brought back up to the surface to be drowned in a flood of words. And since we live at a time when small talk is king, the dead offer no resistance. The role of ghost is imposed upon them and they are bombarded with questions: "Well, now, what was it really like? How did you feel in Minsk and in Kiev and in Kolomea, when the earth, opening up before your eyes, swallowed up your sons and your prayers? What did you think when you saw blood—your own blood—gushing from the bowels of the earth, rising up to the sun? Tell us, speak up, we want to know, to suffer with you, we have a few tears in reserve, they pain us, we want to get rid of them."

One is sometimes reduced to regretting the good old days when this subject, still in the domain of sacred memory, was considered taboo, reserved for the initiates, who spoke of it only with hesitation and fear, always lowering their eyes, and always trembling with humility, knowing themselves unworthy and recognizing the limits of their language, spoken and unspoken.

Now in the name of objectivity, not to mention historical research, everyone takes up the subject without the slightest embarrassment. Accessible to every mind, to every intellect in search of stimulation, this has become the topic of fashionable conversation. Why not? It replaces Brecht, Kafka, and communism, which are now overdone, overworked. In intellectual, or pseudo-intellectual circles, in New York and elsewhere too, no cocktail party can really be called a success unless Auschwitz, sooner or later, figures in the discussion. Excellent remedy for boredom; a good way to ignite passions. Drop the names of a few recent works on this subject, and watch minds come alive, one more brilliant, more arrogant than the next. Psychiatrists, comedians, and novelists, all have their own ideas about the subject, all are clear, each is ready to provide all the answers, to explain all the mysteries: the cold cruelty of the executioner and the cry which strangled the victim, and even the fate that united them to play on the same stage, in the same cemetery. It is as simple as saying hello. As hunger, thirst, and hate. One need only understand history, sociology, politics, psychology, economics; one need know only how to add. And to accept the axiom that everywhere $A+B=C$. If the dead are dead, if so many dead are dead, that is because they desired their own death, they were lured, driven by their own instincts. Beyond the diversity of all the theories, the self-assurance of which cannot but

arouse anger, all unanimously conclude that the victims,
by participating in the executioner's game, in varying degrees shared responsibility.

The novelty of this view cannot fail to be striking.
Until recently, Jews have been held responsible for everything under the sun, the death of Jesus, civil wars, fa-
mines, unemployment, and revolutions: they were
thought to embody evil; now, they are held responsible
for their own death: they embody that death. Thus, we
see that the Jewish problem continues to be a kind of no-
man's land of the mind where anyone can say anything in
any way at all—a game in which everyone wins. Only the
dead are the losers.

And in this game—it is really nothing else—it is quite
easy to blame the dead, to accuse them of cowardice or
complicity (in either the concrete or metaphysical sense
of that term). Now, this game has a humiliating aspect.
To insist on speaking in the name of the dead—and to
say: these are their motivations, these the considerations
that weakened their wills, to speak in their name—this is
precisely to humiliate them. The dead have earned something other than this posthumous humiliation. I never before wholly understood why, in the Jewish faith, anything
that touches corpses is impure. Now I begin to understand.

Let us leave them alone. We will not dig up those
corpses without coffins. Leave them there where they must
forever be and such as they must be: wounds, immea-
surable pain at the very depth of our being. Be content
they do not wake up, that they do not come back to the
earth to judge the living. The day that they would begin
to tell what they have seen and heard, and what they
have taken most to heart, we will not know where to run,
we will stop up our ears, so great will be our fear, so
sharp our shame.

I could understand the desire to dissect history, the
strong urge to close in on the past and the forces shaping

it; nothing is more natural. No question is more important for our generation which is the generation of Auschwitz, or of Hiroshima, tomorrow's Hiroshima. The future frightens us, the past fills us with shame: and these two feelings, like those two events, are closely linked, like cause to effect. It is Auschwitz that will produce Hiroshima, and if the human race should perish by the nuclear bomb, this will be the punishment for Auschwitz, where, in the ashes, the hope of man was extinguished.

And Lot's apprehensive wife, she was right to want to look back and not be afraid to carry the burning of doomed hope. "Know where you come from," the sages of Israel said. But everything depends on the inner attitude of whoever looks back to the beginning: if he does so purely out of intellectual curiosity, his vision will make of him a statue in some salon. Unfortunately, we do not lack statues these days; and what is worse, they speak, as if from the top of the mountain.

And so I read and I listen to these eminent scholars and professors who, having read all the books and confronted all the theories, proclaim their erudition and their power to figure everything out, to explain everything, simply by performing an exercise in classification.

At times, especially at dawn, when I am awakened by the first cry I heard the first night behind barbed wire, a desire comes over me to say to all these illustrious writers who claim to go to the bottom of it all: "I admire you, for I myself stumble when I walk this road; you claim to know everything, there again I admire you: as for me, I know nothing. What is to be done, I know I am still incapable of deciphering—for to do so would be to blaspheme—the frightened smile of that child torn away from his mother and transformed into a flaming torch; nor have I been able, nor will I ever be able, to grasp the shadow which, at that moment, invaded the mother's

eyes. You can, undoubtedly. You are fortunate, I ought
to envy you, but I do not. I prefer to stand on the side of
the child and of the mother who died before they understood the formulas and phraseology which are the basis
of your science."

Also, I prefer to take my place on the side of Job, who
chose questions and not answers, silence and not
speeches. Job never understood his own tragedy which,
after all, was only that of an individual betrayed by God;
to be betrayed by one's fellow men is much more serious.
Yet, the silence of this man, alone and defeated, lasted for
seven days and seven nights; only afterward, when he
identified himself with his pain, did he feel he had earned
the right to question God. Confronted with Job, our silence should extend beyond the centuries to come. And
we dare speak on behalf of our knowledge? We dare say:
"*I know*"? This is how and why victims were victims and
executioners executioners? We dare interpret the agony
and anguish, the self-sacrifice before the faith and the
faith itself of six million human beings, all named Job?
Who are we to judge them?

One of my friends, in the prime of life, spent a night
studying accounts of the holocaust, especially the Warsaw Ghetto. In the morning he looked at himself in the
mirror and saw a stranger: his hair had turned white.
Another lost not his youth but his reason. He plunged
back into the past and remains there still. From time to
time I visit him in his hospital room; we look at one another and we are silent. One day, he shook himself and
said to me: "Perhaps one should learn to cry."

I should envy those scholars and thinkers who pride
themselves on understanding this tragedy in terms of an
entire people; I myself have not yet succeeded in explaining the tragedy of a single one of its sons, no matter
which.

I have nothing against questions: they are useful. What
is more, they alone are. To turn away from them would

be to fail in our duty, to lose our only chance to be able
one day to lead an authentic life. It is against the answers
that I protest, regardless of their basis. Answers: I say
there are none. Each of these theories contains perhaps a
fraction of truth, but their sum still remains beneath and
outside what, in that night, was truth. The events obeyed
no law and no law can be derived from them. The subject
matter to be studied is made up of death and mystery, it
slips away between our fingers, it runs faster than our
perception: it is everywhere and nowhere. Answers only
intensify the question: ideas and words must finally come
up against a wall higher than the sky, a wall of human
bodies extending to infinity.

For more than twenty years, I have been struggling
with these questions. To find one answer or another, nothing is easier: language can mend anything. What the
answers have in common is that they bear no relation to
the questions. I cannot believe that an entire generation
of fathers and sons could vanish into the abyss without
creating, by their very disappearance, a mystery which
exceeds and overwhelms us. I still do not understand
what happened, or how, or why. All the words in all the
mouths of the philosophers and psychologists are not
worth the silent tears of that child and his mother, who
live their own death twice. What can be done? In my
calculations, all the figures always add up to the same
number: six million.

Some time ago, in Jerusalem, I met by chance one of
the three judges in the Eichmann trial. This wise and
lucid man, of uncompromising character, is, to use an
expression dear to Camus, at once a person and a person-
age. He is, in addition, a conscience.

He refused to discuss the technical or legal aspects of
the trial. Having told him that side was of no interest to
me, I asked him the following question:

"Given your role in this trial, you ought to know more about the scope of the holocaust than any living person, more even than those who lived through it in the flesh and in their memory. You have studied all the documents, read all the secret reports, interrogated all the witnesses. Now tell me: do you *understand* this fragment of the past, those few pages of history?"

He shuddered imperceptibly, then, in a soft voice, infinitely humble, he confessed:

"No, not at all. I know the facts and the events that served as their framework; I know how the tragedy unfolded minute by minute, but this knowledge, as if coming from outside, has nothing to do with understanding. There is in all this a portion which will always remain a mystery; a kind of forbidden zone, inaccessible to reason. Fortunately, as it happens. Without that . . ."

He broke off suddenly. Then, with a smile a bit timid, a bit sad, he added:

"Who knows, perhaps that's the gift which God, in a moment of grace, gave to man: it prevents him from understanding everything, thus saving him from madness, or from suicide."

In truth, Auschwitz signifies not only the failure of two thousand years of Christian civilization, but also the defeat of the intellect that wants to find a Meaning—with a capital *M*—in history. What Auschwitz embodied has none. The executioner killed for nothing, the victim died for nothing. No God ordered the one to prepare the stake, nor the other to mount it. During the Middle Ages, the Jews, when they chose death, were convinced that by their sacrifice they were glorifying and sanctifying God's name. At Auschwitz the sacrifices were without point, without faith, without divine inspiration. If the suffering of one human being has any meaning, that of six million has none. Numbers have their own importance; they prove, according to Piotr Rawicz, that God has gone mad.

I attended the Eichmann trial, I heard the prosecutor try to get the witnesses to talk by forcing them to expose themselves and to probe the innermost recesses of their being: Why didn't you resist? Why didn't you attack your assassins when you still outnumbered them?

Pale, embarrassed, ill at ease, the survivors all responded in the same way: "You cannot understand. Anyone who was not there cannot imagine it."

Well, I was there. And I still do not understand. I do not understand that child in the Warsaw Ghetto who wrote in his diary: "I'm hungry, I'm cold; when I grow up I want to be a German, and then I won't be hungry anymore, and I won't be cold anymore."

I still do not understand why I did not throw myself on the Kapo who was beating my father before my very eyes. In Galicia, Jews dug their own graves and lined up, without any trace of panic, at the edge of the trench to await the machine-gun barrage. I do not understand their calm. And that woman, that mother, in the bunker somewhere in Poland, I do not understand her either; her companions smothered her child for fear its cries might betray their presence; that woman, that mother, having lived this scene of biblical intensity, did not go mad. I do not understand her: why, and by what right, and in the name of what, did she not go mad?

I do not know why, but I forbid us to ask her the question. The world kept silent while the Jews were being massacred, while they were being reduced to the state of objects good for the fire; let the world at least have the decency to keep silent now as well. Its questions come a bit late; they should have been addressed to the executioner. Do they trouble us? Do they keep us from sleeping in peace? So much the better. We want to know, to understand, so we can turn the page: is that not true? So we can say to ourselves: the matter is closed and everything is back in order. Do not wait for the dead to come to our rescue. Their silence will survive them.

We have questions? Very good. We do not want to put
them to the executioner—who lives in happiness if not in
glory at home in Germany—well then, pass them on to
those who claim they never participated in the game, to
those who became accomplices through their passivity.
Their "ignorance" of the facts hardly excuses them, it was
willful.

In London and in Washington, in Basel and in Stockholm, high officials had up-to-date information about
every transport carrying its human cargo to the realm of
ashes, to the kingdom of mist. In 1942-1943, they already
possessed photographs documenting the reports; all were
declared "confidential" and their publication prohibited.

Not many voices were raised to warn the executioner
that the day of punishment is at hand; not many voices
were raised to effectively console the victims: that there
will be punishment and that the reign of night is only
temporary.

Perhaps Eichmann was a small man after all. Hitler's
Germany was full of small men like him, all carefully
seeing to it that the extermination machine functioned
well and efficiently. But, large and small, all were sure that
in one regard, that of Nazi policy regarding Jews, they
would have nothing to account for the day after their
defeat: the fate of the Jews interested no one. Someday
they would have to give back the occupied territories and
eventually pay the victors for war damages, that is only
normal. But the Jewish question would not weigh on
them. The Allies could not have cared less about what the
SS did with its Jews. In that area, the Eichmanns could
act with impunity. It is only in this way one can understand how Heinrich Himmler, Grand Master of the death
camps, could, toward the end of the war, have conceived
the possibility of becoming the best negotiator for a separate peace with the western Allies; the fact that his suc-

cessful direction of the annihilation of whole Jewish populations might disqualify him never even crossed his
mind. And when, with feigned irony, Eichmann declared
that no country was interested in saving Jews, he was
telling the truth. Eichmann may have lied about his own
role, but he did not lie about that of the Allies or of the
neutral camp.

In fact, the Germans, known more for maniacal pru-
dence rather than impulsiveness, developed their anti-
Jewish policy step by step, gradually, stopping after each
measure to catch their breath, after each move, to watch
the reactions. There was always a respite between the
different stages, between the Nuremberg laws and the
Kristallnacht, between expropriation and deportation, between the ghettos and liquidation. After each infamy, the
Germans expected a storm of outrage from the free
world; they quickly became aware of their error: they
were allowed to proceed. Of course, here and there, there
were a few speeches, a few editorials, all indignant, but
things stopped there. So, in Berlin, they knew what that
meant. They said to themselves: since we have been
given the green light, we can go on. Moreover, they were
convinced—in all sincerity—that someday other peoples
would be grateful to them for having done the job for
them. Almost all the important Nazis expressed this idea
in their writings; it also appeared in their speeches. They
were killing the Jews for the good of the world, not only
for the good of Germany. After all, the Germans should
not be accused of thinking only of themselves.

I maintain that by forceful action, only once, by taking
a stand without ambiguities, the free world would have
been able to force the Germans to draw back, or at least
to plan on a smaller scale. It is conceivable that for Berlin
the absence of such action could only have meant a tacit
agreement, unacknowledged, on the part of the Allied
powers. One need only glance through the newspapers of
the period to become disgusted with the human adven-

ture on this earth: the phenomenon of the concentration camps, despite its horror and its overwhelming ramifications, took up less space, on the whole, than did ordinary traffic accidents.

It would be a mistake to believe the inmates of the camps were ignorant of this. Knowing themselves abandoned, excluded, rejected by the rest of humanity, their walk to death, as haughty as it was submissive, became an act of lucidity, of protest, and not of acceptance and weakness.

Yes: the transport of which I was a part did not rebel on the night of our arrival. What must be added is that the young men spoke also of the necessity of alerting the outside world: naïve, they still believed the Germans were doing their work secretly, like thieves, that the Allies knew nothing about it, for if they knew, the massacre would stop immediately. "We will fight," they said. "We will break this silence and the world will know that Auschwitz is a reality." I shall never forget the old man who, in a calm voice, terribly calm, answered them: "You are young and brave, my children; you still have a lot to learn. The world knows, no need to inform it. It knew before you did, but it doesn't care, it won't lose a minute thinking about our fate. Your revolt will have no bearing, no echo." The old man spoke without bitterness; he stated the facts. He was Polish and two years before had seen his family slaughtered: I do not know how he managed to escape and to slip across two frontiers before arriving among us, a refugee. "Save your strength for later," he told our young men. "Don't waste it." But they were persistent. "Even if you are right," they rejoined, "even if what you say is true, that doesn't change the situation. Let us prove our courage and our dignity, let us show these murderers and the world that Jews know how to die like free men, not like hunched-up invalids." "As a lesson, I like that," the old man's voice reached me. "But they don't deserve it."

Then we all held our heads up high and murmuring the words of the *Kaddish* we marched ahead, almost like conquerors, toward the gates of death where the elegant physician Dr. Josef Mengele—white gloves, monocle, and the rest—accomplished the sacred ritual of selection, of separating those who would live from those who would die.

The old man had seen things as they were. Had the Jews been able to think they had allies outside, men who did not look the other way, perhaps they might have acted differently. But the only people interested in the Jews were the Germans. The others preferred not to look, not to hear, not to know. The solitude of the Jews, caught in the clutches of the beast, has no precedent in history. It was total. Death guarded all the exits.

It was worse than the Middle Ages. Then, driven from Spain, the Jews were welcomed in Holland. Persecuted in one country, they were invited to another, given time to take heart again. But during the Hitler era the conspiracy against them seemed universal. The English closed off the gates of Palestine, the Swiss accepted only the rich—and later the children—while the poor and the adult, their right to life denied, were driven back into the darkness. "Even if I had been able to sell a million Jews, who would have bought them?" asked Eichmann, not without sarcasm, alluding to the Hungarian episode. Here again he was telling the truth. "What do you want us to do with a million Jews?" echoed the honorable Lord Moyne, British ambassador to Cairo. It is as though every country—and not only Germany—had decided to see the Jew as a kind of subhuman species, an unnecessary being, not like others; his disappearance did not count, did not weigh on the conscience. He was a being to whom the concept of human brotherhood did not apply, a being whose death did not diminish us, a being with whom one did not identify. One could therefore do with him what one would, without violating the laws of the spirit; one could take away his freedom and joy without betraying the ideal of man. I often wonder what the world's reaction would have been had the Nazi machine ground up and burned day after day, not twenty thousand Jews, but twenty thousand Christians. It is better not to think about that too much.

If I dwell so long on the culpability of the world, it is not to lessen that of the Germans, nor to "explain" the behavior of their victims. We tend to forget.

The fact, for example, that in the spring of 1944 we, in Transylvania, knew nothing about what was happening in Germany is proof of the world's guilt. We listened to the short-wave radio, from London and Moscow: not a single broadcast warned us not to leave with the transports, not one disclosed the existence, not even the name of Auschwitz. In 1943, when she read three lines in a Hungarian newspaper concerning the Warsaw Ghetto uprising, my mother remarked: "But why did they do it? Why didn't they wait *peacefully* for the end of hostilities?" Had we known what was happening there, we might have been able to flee, to hide: the Russian front was only thirty kilometers away. But we were kept in the dark.

At the risk of offending, it must be emphasized that the victims suffered more, and more profoundly, from the indifference of the onlookers than from the brutality of the executioner. The cruelty of the enemy would have been incapable of breaking the prisoner; it was the silence of those he believed to be his friends—cruelty more cowardly, more subtle—which broke his heart.

There was no longer anyone on whom to count: even in the camps this became evident. *"From now on we shall live in the wilderness, in the void: blotted out of history."* It was this conviction which poisoned the desire to live. If this is the world we were born into, why cling to it? If this is the human society we come from—and are now abandoned by—why seek to return?

At Auschwitz, not only man died, but also the idea of man. To live in a world where there is nothing anymore, where the executioner acts as god, as judge—many wanted no part of it. It was its own heart the world incinerated at Auschwitz.

to 194

Let no one misinterpret. I speak without hatred, without bitterness. If at times I do not succeed in containing my anger, it is because I find it shocking if not indecent that one must plead to protect the dead. For that is the issue: they are being dug up in order to be pilloried. The questions asked of them are only reproaches. They are being blamed, these corpses, for having acted as they did: they should have played their roles differently, if only to reassure the living who might thus go on believing in the nobility of man. We do not like those men and women for whom the sky became a common grave. We speak of them without pity, without compassion, without love. We juggle their thousand ways of dying as if performing intellectual acrobatics: our heart is not in it. More than that: we despise them. For the sake of convenience, and also to satisfy our mania to classify and define everything, we make some distinctions: between the Germans and the *Judenrat*, between the Kapos and the ghetto police, between the nameless victim and the victim who obtained a reprieve for a week, for a month. We judge them and we hand out certificates for good or bad conduct. We detest some more than others: we are on the other side of the wall, and we know exactly the degree of guilt of each of them. On the whole, they inspire our disgust rather than our anger.

That is what I reproach us for: our boundless arrogance in thinking we know everything. And that we have the right to pass judgment on an event which should, on the contrary, serve as proof that we are poor, and that our dreams are barren—when they are not bloody.

I plead for the dead and I do not say they are innocent; that is neither my intention nor aim. I say simply we have no right to judge them; to confer innocence upon them is already to judge them. I saw them die and if I feel the need to speak of guilt, it is always of my own that I speak. I saw them go away and I remained behind. Often I do not forgive myself for that.

Of course, in the camps I saw men conquered, weak, cruel. I do not hesitate to admit I hated them, they frightened me; for me, they represented a danger greater than the Germans. Yes, I have known sadistic Kapos; yes, I have seen Jews, a savage gleam burning in their eyes, whipping their own brothers. But, though they played the executioner's game, they died as victims. When I think about it, I am still astonished that so few souls were lost, so few hearts poisoned, in that kingdom of the night, where one breathed only hate, contempt, and self-disgust. What would have become of me had I stayed in the camps longer, five years, or seven, or twelve? I have been trying to answer that question for more than twenty years and at times, after a sleepless night, I am afraid of the answer. But many people are not afraid. These questions, which are discussed as one might discuss a theorem or a scientific problem, do not frighten us. For that, too, I reproach us.

Since the end of the nightmare I search the past, whose prisoner I shall no doubt forever remain. I am afraid, but I still pursue my quest. The further I go, the less I understand. Perhaps there is nothing to understand.

On the other hand, the further I go, the more I learn of the scope of the betrayal by the world of the living against the world of the dead. I take my head in my hands and I think: it is insanity, that is the explanation, the only conceivable one. When so great a number of men carry their indifference to such an extreme, it becomes sickness, it resembles madness.

Otherwise how to explain the Roosevelts, the Churchills, the Eisenhowers, who never expressed their indignation? How to explain the silence of the Pope? How to explain the failure of certain attempts in London, in Washington, to obtain from the Allies an aerial bombardment of the death factories, or at least of the railway lines leading to them?

One of the saddest episodes of that war, not lacking in sad episodes, had as hero a Polish Jewish leader exiled in London: to protest the inaction of the Allies, and also to alert public opinion, Arthur Ziegelbaum, member of the "National Committee to Free Poland," put a bullet through his head in broad daylight in front of the entrance to the House of Commons. In his will he expressed his hope that his protest would be heard.

He was quickly forgotten, his death proved useless. Had he believed his refusal to live among men voluntarily blind would move them, he had been wrong. Ziegelbaum dead or Ziegelbaum living: to those hearts of stone it was all the same. For them he was only a Polish Jew talking about Jews and living their agony; for them he might just as well have perished over there, with the others. Arthur Ziegelbaum died for nothing. Life went on, so did the war: against the Axis powers, which continued their own war against the Jews. And the world stopped up its ears and lowered its eyes. Sometimes the newspapers printed a small item: the Ghetto of Lodz had been liquidated, the number of European Jews massacred already exceeded two or three million. This news was published as if these were normal events, almost without comment, without anguish. It seemed normal that Jews should be killed by the Nazis. Never had the Jewish people been so alone.

The more I search, the more reasons I find for losing hope. I am often afraid to reopen this Pandora's box, there are always the newly guilty to emerge from it. Is there no bottom to this evil box? No.

I repeat: hatred is no solution. There would be too many targets. The Hungarians put more passion than did the Germans into the persecution of Jews; the Rumanians displayed more savagery than the Germans; the Slovaks, the Poles, the Ukrainians: they hunted down Jews cunningly, as if with love. Perhaps I should hate them, it would cure me. But I am incapable. Were hatred a solution, the survivors, when they came out of the camps, would have had to burn down the whole world.

Now almost everywhere I am told: you mustn't bear a grudge against us, we didn't know, we didn't believe it, we were powerless to do anything. If these justifications suffice to assuage people's consciences, too bad for them. I could answer that they did not want to know, that they refused to believe, that they could have forced their governments to break the conspiracy of silence. But that would open the door to discussion. It is too late, in any case: the time for discussion is past.

Now, I shall simply ask: is it any surprise that the Jews did not choose resistance? And die fighting like soldiers for the victory of their cause? But what victory and what cause?

Let me reveal a secret, one among a thousand, about why Jews did not resist: to punish us, to prepare a vengeance for us for later. We were not worth their sacrifice. If, in every town and every village, in the Ukraine and in Galicia, in Hungary and in Czechoslovakia, Jews formed endless nightly processions and marched on to eternity as if carrying within themselves a pure joy, one which heralds the approach of ecstasy, it is precisely to reveal to us the ultimate truth about those who are sacrificed on the margins of history. In staying alive, at that price, we deserve neither salvation nor atonement. Nor do we even deserve that lesson of solemn dignity and lofty courage which, in spite of everything, in their own way, they gave us by making their way toward death, staring it full in the face, point blank, their heads high in the joy of bearing this strength, this pride within themselves.

Let us, therefore, not make an effort to understand, but rather to lower our eyes and not understand. Every rational explanation would be more esoteric than if it were mystical. Not to understand the dead is a way of paying them an ancient debt; it is the only way to ask their pardon.

I have before me a photograph, taken by a German officer fond of souvenirs, of a father who, an instant before the burst of rifle fire, was still speaking calmly to his son, while pointing to the sky. Sometimes I think I hear his dreamy voice: "You see, my son, we are going to die and the sky is beautiful. Do not forget there is a connection between these two facts." Or perhaps: "We are going to die, my son, yet the sky, so serene, is not collapsing in an end-of-the-world crash. Do you hear its silence? Listen to it, you must not forget it." It occurs to me that were I to ask him a question, any question, that same father would answer me. But I bury my eyes in what remains of him and I am silent.

Just as I am silent every time the image comes to my mind of the Rebbe in Warsaw who stood erect, unyielding, unconquerable, before a group of SS; they were amusing themselves by making him suffer, by humiliating him; he suffered, but did not let himself be humiliated. One of them, laughing, cut off his beard, but the Rebbe stared right into his eyes without flinching; there was pain in his expression, but also defiance, the expression of a man stronger than evil, even when evil is triumphant, stronger than death, even when death assumes the face of a comedian playing a farce—the expression of a man who owes nothing to anyone, not even to God.

I have long since carried that expression buried within me, I have not been able to part with it, I no longer want to part with it, as though wanting always to remember there are still, there will always be, somewhere in the world, expressions I will never understand. And when such an expression lights upon me, at the dinner table, at a concert, or beside a happy woman, I give myself up to it in silence.

For the older I grow, the more I know that we can do

little for the dead; the least we can do is to leave them
alone, not project our own guilt onto them. We like to
think the dead have found eternal rest: let them be. It is
dangerous to wake them. They, too, have questions, questions equal to our own.

My plea is coming to an end, but it would be incomplete if I said nothing about the armed assaults which, in
spite of what the prosecution may think, Jews did carry
out against the Germans. If I have difficulty understanding how multitudes went to their death without defending themselves, that difficulty becomes insurmountable
when it comes to understanding those of their companions who chose to fight.

How, in the ghettos and camps, they were able to find
the means to fight when the whole world was against
them—that will always remain a mystery.

For those who claim that all the Jews submitted to
their murderers, to fate, in common cowardice or common resignation, those people do not know what they are
saying or—what is worse—knowingly falsify the facts
only to illustrate a sociological theory, or to justify a
morbid hatred which is always self-hatred.

In truth, there was among the victims an active elite of
fighters composed of men and women and children who,
with pitiful means, stood up against the Germans. They
were a minority, granted. But is there any society where
the active elite is not a minority? Such groups existed in
Warsaw, in Bialystok, in Grodno, and—God alone knows
how—even in Treblinka, in Sobivor, and in Auschwitz.
Authenticated documents and eye-witness accounts do
exist, relating the acts of war of those poor desperadoes;
reading them, one does not know whether to rejoice with
admiration or to weep with rage. One wonders: but how
did they do it, those starving youngsters, those hunted
men, those battered women, how were they able to confront, with weapons in hand, the Nazi army, which at
that time seemed invincible, marching from victory to

victory? Where did they take their sheer physical endurance, their moral strength? What was their secret and
what is its name?

We say: weapons in hand. But what weapons? They
had hardly any. They had to pay in pure gold for a single
revolver. In Bialystok, the legendary Mordecai Tenen-
baum-Tamaroff, leader of the ghetto resistance, describes
in his journal—miraculously rediscovered—the moment
he obtained the first rifle, the first ammunition: twenty-
five bullets. "Tears came to my eyes. I felt my heart burst
with joy." It was thus with one rifle and twenty-five bullets that he and his companions were going to contain the
vast onslaught of the German army. It is easy to imagine
what might have happened had every warrior in every
ghetto obtained one rifle.

All the underground networks in the occupied countries received arms, money, and radio equipment from
London, and secret agents came regularly to teach them
the art of sabotage: they felt themselves organically
linked to the outside world. In France or Norway a member of the resistance who was caught could comfort himself with the thought that somewhere in that town as well
as on the other shore, there were people who feared for
his life, who lived in anxiety because of him, who would
move heaven and earth to save him: his acts registered
somewhere, left traces, marks of sorrow, produced results.
But the Jews were alone: only they were alone.

They alone did not receive help or encouragement; neither arms nor messages were sent them; they were not
spoken to, no one was concerned with them; they did not
exist. They cried for help, but the appeals they issued by
radio or by mail fell on deaf ears. Cut off from the world,
from the war itself, the Jewish fighters participated, fully
aware they were not wanted, they had already been written off; they threw themselves into battle knowing they
could count on no one, help would never arrive, they
would receive no support, there would be no place to

retreat. And yet, with their backs to the burning wall, they defied the Germans. Some battles are won even when they are lost.

Yes, competent elite existed even at Sobivor, where they organized an escape; at Treblinka, where they revolted; and at Auschwitz, where they blew up the crematoria. The Auschwitz insurgents attempted an escape, but in the struggle with the SS, who obviously had an advantage of superiority in weapons and men, all were killed. Later the Germans arrested the four young Jewish girls from Warsaw who had obtained the explosives for the insurgents. They were tortured, condemned to death, and hanged at a public ceremony. They died without fear. The oldest was sixteen, the youngest twelve.

We can only lower our heads and be silent. And end this sickening posthumous trial which intellectual acrobats everywhere are carrying on against those whose death numbs the mind. Do we want to understand? There is no longer anything to understand. Do we want to know? There is nothing to know anymore. It is not by playing with words and the dead that we will understand and know. Quite the contrary. As the ancients said: "Those who know do not speak; those who speak do not know."

But we prefer to speak and to judge. We wish to be strong and invulnerable. The lesson of the holocaust—if there is any—is that our strength is only illusory, and that in each of us is a victim who is afraid, who is cold, who is hungry. Who is also ashamed.

The Talmud teaches man never to judge his friend until he has been in his place. But, for the world, the Jews are not friends. They have never been. Because they had no friends they are dead.

So, learn to be silent.